How to Sell
Vintage & Gold Jewelry Online

A snarky, opinionated guide to
selling smalls & all.

By Micki Suzanne

Bodhi Press

Copyright © 2013 Micki Suzanne

Bodhi Press
ISBN-13: 978-0978739324
ISBN-10: 0978739329

Jewelry has been a powerful tool
for self-expression for thousands of years.

It tells the world who we are, who we love and
which gods (or saints) protect us.

It's a measure of success, bought and worn in good times;
hidden away or sold in the marketplace in bad times.

Our times are difficult and our marketplace is online.

This little book is a casual overview of my processes,
told in simple steps with stories and examples.

Skim it to get a general sense for how selling online
might work for you; or use the Table of Contents to
zero in on the information you need.

The methods I recommend for jewelry apply to
smalls and other collectibles as well.

Chapter 16 offers tips for selling large antiques.

Chapter 14 – Buying Online to Sell Online – is
important for people who would like to
buy and sell without leaving home.

My goal is that this book will pay for itself
MANY times over.

Micki Suzanne

DEDICATION

To the original glamour girl,
my grandmother Edla Sofia Bolen

And glamour girls to be,
my granddaughters Emma and Ella

CONTENTS

CHAPTER 1: CRISIS

eBay saved my ass in 2012. Business was as slow as client payments. Bills were rolling in; mortgage, insurance and association fees were all due at the same time.

Forced to choose between my tropical townhouse on stilts and a tragic return to the cold gray north, I panicked and did the unthinkable; I surrendered good jewelry to the gold buyers.

I chose an established jewelry store, hoping "reputable jewelers" would rip me off *a little less* than the skeevy fly-by-nights.

I slunk into the gleaming store with two plastic bags. One contained broken jewelry and a heavy 14k gold sand dollar; the other contained a few unmarked favorites. At the very least I would know which of the unmarked pieces were gold.

I was especially anxious about this amethyst ring;

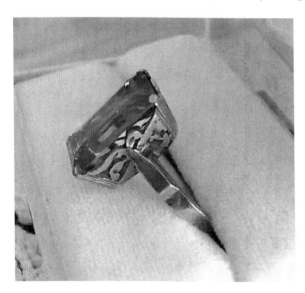

I told the dull young man I wasn't sure about selling it.

He grunted acknowledgment as he turned to walk my valuables back to the guys with microscopes and scales.

I watched as they weighed my fate behind the glass.

A few minutes later he returned and said *everything* was 14k. I sacrificed this sand dollar and a few other pieces for a fraction of their value.

He offered $55 for the amethyst ring, but I kept it – and my favorites – knowing I could do much better online.

Hundreds could have been a thousand or more if I had taken the time to sell my gold jewelry on eBay.

In November I started listing. Everything had changed since the last time I sold online. The economy was down, but gold was up; that was a good thing.

I priced the amethyst ring at $250 in eBay's Buy it Now with Best Offer format. I wound up accepting an offer of $220 – *four times what the gold buyers had offered!*

Over the holidays I sold another $3,000 in jewelry. I had hoped to keep my best for Emma and Ella, but I needed the money.

(14k gold bracelet, sold 2012)

I took comfort in the fact that my treasures were in – and on – the hands of some very nice people.

I still had some jewelry online, but it didn't *need* to sell. My payments were up to date and I had enough money to cover emergency vet bills.

I walked away from the holidays thinking "everyone should know how to do this."

This book (naturally) features jewelry I've sold or am selling. A few of the photos are older, but most are recent and some are live.

My casual tone and grammar are real too.

That's who I am, that's me writing to you as a friend. If eBay helps me survive this economy, odds are good it can help you too.

HELPING PEOPLE SELL

Selling online is a valuable skill. If you know what you're doing, passion for vintage jewelry and collectibles can be a financial lifeline in this crap economy.

When I say "eBay" I mean any reputable online sales or auction service. I've tried a few of the others, but they don't compare to the original.

I've been selling antiques and collectibles since the 90s. I rented space in antique malls, got screwed at auction and eventually made enough money as a marketing writer to open my own shop.

(My antique shop in Michigan)

The place was half hangout and half classroom.

People parked near the front door and stumbled in with boxes full of prized possessions. It was heartbreaking; some had lost their health and/or their jobs. Others were struggling to get by on disability.

They were almost always desperate for money. I couldn't bring myself to send them away with "Sorry – I don't sell that type of merchandise."

They'd ask if I could recommend a nearby dealer. I explained that shop owners make a living by paying very little and selling for as much as they can. I *didn't* warn them that a few bad eggs are *masterful* liars who insult when they buy and deceive when they sell.

I didn't want to see people get ripped off. I knew they were better off selling on their own; they just needed to learn how.

I had up to date price guides on my shelves and internet at the ready. I taught them to check values and establish realistic prices. Their questions were the inspiration for my first book.

I understood their apprehension because I never wanted to sell online either! I've been *buying* online since 1998, but selling seemed like too much work. It meant taking photographs, writing descriptions, shipping and the rest of it.

Finally illness and job loss forced me to dive in. To my surprise, selling online was – and is – a hoot. And when you enjoy a thing, you tend to get good at it.

In 2006 eBay invited me to fly out to California to become a member of their Voices of the Community. I thought the email was a hoax.

My stent for IV antibiotics had just been removed and I was still spacy from Lyme disease, *but what an opportunity!*

I returned a zealot – physically and mentally weak but emotionally high on eBay stores. I was anxious to share what I had learned with my customers, dealer buddies and online support group of chronically ill friends.

My first book

It took six months to write *Sick Mick's Guide to Selling Antiques and Collectibles*. I hadn't looked at it since; but I did receive emails.

I'd written so much about Lyme disease, some readers recognized their symptoms and sought appropriate treatment.

One woman had been living with a diagnosis of MS; she wrote that she hoped to be out of her wheelchair in time for her son's wedding. *(Gulp)*

A local antique shop carried the book for a while. The owner told me a customer with leukemia said it gave her hope that she could still be productive despite illness. *That was my intent.*

But when I picked it up again last year, I about died of embarrassment.

I was obviously very sick and scattered when I wrote it. I'm much better now – *really I am* – and this chronic recession is the *perfect* time for a do-over.

Because sick or not, most everyone is hurting.

What about you?

If you've been watching Antiques Roadshow you know what was hot has cooled and some of the things we once snubbed as inconsequential – silver jewelry and gold-filled items – have appreciated in value.

(14k gold bracelet, sold online in 2012)

If you have gold jewelry, don't even *think* about selling to the gold buyers.

I'll show you how to sell it online.

CHAPTER 2: MY STORY

Gram's big black Buick took us hundreds of miles north to Michigan's Upper Peninsula. The signal under the left fin flashed our intentions and we drove west a few hundred more.

We didn't know what to expect, but there it was; my Finnish great grandparents' farmhouse – tall, sad and alone on Himanka Hill. Gram was born there. I'd heard all the stories. I wanted to find a loose board and crawl inside, but they said the floors weren't safe.

Mom suggested we go digging instead. "You know, they always used to throw trash out back. We might be able to find dishes or bottles or something."

That could be fun. I dug in the sand, saw a lip and pulled gently. They were all broken. After 30 minutes I was getting frustrated. Finally I tugged and the sand surrendered a complete bottle in a shape I had never seen.

The heavens opened and angels sang.

Later that afternoon we visited an old gray woman in an old gray house with old gray wood floors, walls and ceilings. Gram was happy at the opportunity to "speak Finn" again. They talked about growing up in the U.P.; about who had moved and who had died.

I wasn't listening. I was staring at a strange crab-like insect on the floor. It stood flat and defiant, like a guard bug.

When we left, Gram and Mom talked about ticks. It didn't register as anything that would ever matter to *me*, so I ignored them. It's funny how things can come back to bite you.

But it was a good day, a happy day. I didn't have a lot of those.

Growing up JW

Mom could have passed for Marilyn Monroe's sister and her platinum blonde hair was the real deal. When I was two she became a Jehovah's Witness and set about converting the rest of the family.

It was a strange way to grow up. On Tuesday nights we had hour long book studies at someone's house. But mostly we were at the Kingdom Hall for two hours on Thursday nights and two hours on Sunday mornings. *It **never** stopped being excruciating.*

As a small child I remember standing on the bolt-secured folding seat to gawk at the well-dressed ladies behind me – only to lose my footing and be gobbled whole by the chair.

It was worth the humiliation as their beaded purses held Juicy Fruit gum or Life Savers; and their jewelry – well, it was *unforgettable.*

(With Gram at my uncle's first wedding)

On weekends they had me out pounding doors with dimpled fists, too small to reach the doorbells. As I grew I gained a sense for our intrusiveness.

Sunday mornings were the worst; cranky men with hangovers and hairy bellies answered the doors in their skivvies.

JW children didn't have birthdays or Christmas. We were taught to remain seated during the national anthem and pledge of allegiance; so there was no blending in at school.

It was just as well, we weren't *supposed* to play with non-believers; *but I did.* It was hard to understand why God would destroy my friends and their parents when Armageddon came.

(With Mom at Greenfield Village)

Mom got a job at Hudson's Department Store, where she worked her way up from the juice bar to manager of the fabric department.

Discounted remnants were manna from heaven as sewing was the only way we could afford to build fine wardrobes.

I was 15 when the elders announced a three week tour of Europe and Scandinavia. The Kingdom Hall *buzzed* with excitement. *Travel was for rich people, certainly not us!*

But Gram was intrigued by the idea. She wanted to meet our relatives in Finland and she didn't want to go alone. Mom made financial sacrifices to pay my expenses and Gram and I were on our way.

We flew from Detroit to New York City; then across the Atlantic Ocean to London's Heathrow Airport — hallowed ground where the Beatles departed and returned, where itty-bitty city yards overflowed with flowers. In Ireland we saw very little because of the fog.

In Finland we took a train north from Helsinki to Nivala. I could see why Gram's parents moved to Michigan's Upper Peninsula; the landscape and climate were *exactly* the same.

In Sweden a tour director talked about people who prayed to Satan because he answered faster than Jesus.

In Scotland we stayed at an ancient place on the North Sea. We walked the shore under a midnight sun, pulled heavy drapes to darken our room and sank deep into lush featherbeds with beefy bedding. Gram giggled – "Snug as a bug in a rug!"

(From Wikipedia; Edinburgh Castle by Kim Traynor)

I stood in the massive echoing halls of Edinburgh Castle as figures from an ancient tapestry gazed down upon me. *I was overcome by a soul tingling sense of psychic connection.*

I came home transformed, completely smitten by anything "weird and old." I started spending my babysitting money at flea markets in East Detroit and Warren – near the *8-Mile* of Eminem fame.

My first furniture purchase was a folk art chair; the back had been carved and painted to look like the toes on a right foot. It was hideous but I *loved* it.

Gram tempered my crazy by teaching me to shop. All of our expeditions featured a pleasant lunch and quality time at the jewelry counters of better department stores.

I still have the first garnet ring I purchased with her in the 60s.

Serial marrier

The years between then and now read like fiction. My first husband was a suitable match made within the framework of the cult.

Honorable JW teens weren't supposed to date for sport; we were to find a respectable mate and marry.

His father was a prominent elder, his mother an obedient JW wife. His childhood was tougher than mine; *he didn't have one.* They rushed their only child from diapers and booties to wingtips and briefcases.

My "going steady" ring was a pearl in silver (?). When it fell out, an impatient jeweler roughly informed me it was "too cheap to fix."

I sewed my own wedding gown, his father officiated and my aunt said I was the only sad bride she had ever seen.

Well, I didn't see much to look forward to.

Pious JW newlyweds lived like paupers so they could dedicate their lives to warning people about Armageddon; but we had already been banging on doors *all of our lives*.

The elders said the end would arrive by 1975; but the Bible said no man knows the day or the hour. *What made them think they knew?* I was getting pissed.

The righteous would be persecuted; babies would be torn from mothers' arms, so *it was best not to have one*.

Shawn's birth was my defining moment. There was no way I would let my baby die if he needed a blood transfusion; I knew people who had. And I wasn't going to raise him with that joyless, spirit crushing end of times mentality.

A friendly divorce preserved the relationship and quitting the church brought me closer to God. Shawn was only four, but he never forgot the time before Christmas.

1975 came and the world did not end; *it began*. I was hired by an industrial film company, where I worked with Broadway producers, photographers and *writers*. I spent years typing their scripts, never dreaming one day I would be invited to join their ranks.

John Forsythe and Don Knotts called to talk to my boss; they were old friends. Bill Bixby did magic for one of our shows; I met him on set.

Shawn and I reveled in our first birthdays and holidays. I filled our apartment with antique oak furniture and 100 year old Victorian prints of children, dogs and angels. I wore art nouveau jewelry I found at flea markets.

Too soon it was the 80s, all big hair, shoulder pads and MTV. My second husband owned and trained racehorses. He inspired me with his ability to achieve *anything* he set his mind to.

My engagement ring was as big as a skating rink and my costume jewelry was straight out of Dynasty.

Shawn and I were welcomed into his home, but my antiques were banished to the basement. It's not like my furniture wasn't good enough; he just wanted to call *all* the shots. That gets old fast.

Mid-decade I saw an opening for an entry-level marketing writer for Jeep and Burger King and went for it. My dream of a writing career began as the marriage began to end.

I was writing some of the first web marketing (Prodigy) when I met Art. He was love at first sight – a tall, beautiful Catholic boy with sad eyes. He had grown wealthy over three, four and more martini lunches.

The first time I walked into his house I *gasped;* we were a match made in the Antiques Roadshow. He proposed on a Caribbean cruise, bought me breathtaking jewelry and took me on adventures I'll never forget.

I even had time to play. I began selling my antiques at malls in Lexington and Royal Oak. Soon I was picking and buying at flea markets from Detroit to Sanilac County.

Playtime ended when a head hunter called to tell me about a position with a company I greatly admired. The internet was exploding and they needed a web-savvy writer for Chrysler.

I learned about exciting new technologies and started buying stock; my first was some *online flea market* called eBay.

The harder Art drank, the harder I worked. The harder I worked, the more money I made; and there were promotions. Soon I was earning enough money to buy a Victorian cottage on the St. Clair River.

The first night we "camped" on the floor of the waterfront sitting room and felt the *thump/thump/thump* heartbeat of freighters as they passed in the mist.

I wanted Art to love the house; I wanted it to save us. But the bottle (almost) always wins.

Shawn had his own family by the time I found myself alone in the house with semi-dangerous Sass, my big black Bouvier. Bats flew laps in my round Victorian bedroom; they chattered behind the walls as I logged on, but I didn't care. I wanted to grow old and die there.

I grew roses in my waterfront garden. I filled the rooms with my best antiques and continued to buy more. My spares went to a nice bright space I rented at the Antiques Warehouse.

The only problem was the distance to work. When offered a similar position for a lesser company much closer to home, I made a leap of faith; and began cursing my optimism.

Fortunately I found strong shoulders to lean on. I used to joke that Randy was the best husband I never had. He was earthy, absolutely outrageous and a savvy businessman.

When a dealer told me about a Victorian property he thought I'd like, we went to take a look. It had an era-correct retail space on the main level and a spacious upper apartment with panoramic river views.

I opened an antique shop, hired a dealer to run it weekdays and I worked most weekends. Before I knew it, I was juggling my first business, two mortgages, and a job where alpha males treated well-paid women with open contempt.

As the oldest female in the herd, I was wearing a bulls-eye. Panic attacks set in. I sat in my van every morning praying my pulse back to normal. The receptionist always waved me in with an "I feel your pain" expression.

Weekends with Randy were my salvation. He had a hot tub, swimming pool and five acres of woods.

One Sunday I should have been poolside catching late rays, but no – I was cranked back in his bony blue La-Z-Boy watching Sex and the City.

Sassy ambled over, circled three times and curled up at my feet. She had been out back chasing deer. Her soft wavy fur carried the parasitic freeloader that would steal my health, my wealth and my man.

"The thing" I clawed from my thigh that day was a deer tick; but I didn't know. I *wouldn't* know for a long time. It was round and hard as a bullet with my blood.

Years of crushing illness and brain fog passed without income or diagnosis. I literally kissed my house good-bye and cried through a red light on my way back to Randy's.

It was time to rethink the spoils of failed relationships; the skating rink was the first to go. I was freaked about putting something so valuable on eBay. Emma was checking the pool filters for trapped frogs the day it sold.

I vaguely remember putting the big pear cut diamond in her sticky little palm and apologizing that it should have been hers one day.

Then I cleaned it, insured it and shipped it to Texas. The new owner was ecstatic. I was encouraged; *I could do this.*

So can you.

So there you have it. I've survived one cult, 3 husbands and Lyme disease. In 2006 I said good-bye to my family, rented a 17' U-Haul and drove the last of my possessions south to the sunshine and Gulf breezes of Southwest Florida.

My symptoms are *much* better here.

(Cuddling a parrot at Skunk Ape HQ in Ochopee in 2009)

My Florida family is a Lhasa rescue girl who's afraid of storms and a grumpy Oreo Shih Tzu who springs to life all chompy with piranha teeth after midnight.

Freelance writing projects have paid (most of) the bills and eBay is my safety net.

When work is steady, I search eBay for estate jewelry bargains. When work is slow, I sell.

CHAPTER 3: SELLING ON EBAY

I challenge you to find any legal home-based business that produces this much fun, drama and potential for profit.

How will you sell?

You may choose to join the ranks of what I call "the dollar dealers" – people who generate steady income by sending hundreds of items through eBay auctions with rock bottom starting prices.

On the upside:

- Quantity, speed and efficiency result in decent per-hour earnings.
- They have so many followers their better pieces sell at good prices.
- Some manage to sell trinkets I've thrown out.

On the downside:

- Some forgo item identification and full descriptions in order to list, sell and ship quickly.
- Their photos have an "assembly line" look.
- Selling to cheapskates seems to affect their feedback; there is no way you can sell thousands of items without dealing with crankasses.

I admire their tenacity, but I would rather take my time and sell better merchandise at a fair profit.

My selling preferences and process

I sell the way I buy. That is, I am only attracted to the traditional auction format and Buy it Now with Best Offer. (eBay calls it "Buy it Now *or* Best Offer." For the purposes of this book, "with" seems a little less confusing.)

I avoid any auction that has a reserve. I find them exasperating.

My process involves:

- Choosing the pieces I want to sell based on season or holiday.
- Researching when necessary.
- Checking current prices – especially gold and silver.
- Writing thorough descriptions with all relevant search words.
- Taking great photos.
- Listing my items.
- Monitoring activity on my listings.
- Answering questions promptly.
- Shipping like a pro.
- Leaving feedback.

Some items will attract "watchers" within moments of being listed. Watchers are no guarantee your item will sell, but it's encouraging to know people are interested.

About My eBay

My eBay is your base of operations, it's everything you're watching, buying and selling. Views/Watchers (within All Selling) will tell you how many people are watching your items. If you don't have watchers, you may have a problem.

Selling after a long absence

In November of 2012 I eased back into the natural rhythms of listing for the holidays. By Thanksgiving I had listed 25 items and most had watchers. Within days I was getting offers on some of my Buy it Now items.

Can you see yourself doing this?

SIGN UP NOW

Go to eBay www.ebay.com and click Register.

All you *truly* need is a computer and a digital camera or eBay's selling app for your smartphone or iPad.

When you sign up it will ask you for an eBay user ID; this is your eBay name, what sellers see when you buy and buyers see when you sell. Play with it; one unforgettable seller was "deadguystuff."

I wanted mine to describe what I sell, so I'm "greatestatejewelry."

Follow the directions on the site. I could step you through it, but eBay *constantly* tweaks the way they do things; same goes for PayPal.

How eBay fees are paid

You establish your automatic payment method when you set up your selling account. My fees are automatically deducted from my PayPal account, with my debit card/checking account as backup.

Sign up for PayPal

Your chances of selling are better with PayPal because:

- There is no charge to buyers.
- Customers don't need a PayPal account; the system accepts any credit card or currency.
- PayPal Purchase Protection guarantees their transactions.

PayPal does charge sellers a fixed percentage and transaction fee on every sale, so factor that into your prices.

Go to www.paypal.com and click Sign Up; or you can call them to set up over the phone.

I tend to use PayPal like a second bank account:

- eBay sales are deposited to my account within minutes.
- All recent deposits, transactions and transfers are recorded.
- It can be used to pay – or receive payments from – people and businesses off eBay. All you need to send or receive funds is the email address associated with the PayPal account.)

Funds transfer to my bank account within about three days.

PayPal seller tools

PayPal has added PayPal Here – a system that gives you the ability to take credit and debit card payments via your iPhone, iPad or Android device. (It simply plugs into whatever you're using.)

According to PayPal.com, the interest rate is low (currently 2.7% per swipe) "with no setup or monthly fees." This is something to consider if you decide to do flea markets or shows.

Beware of spoof, scam, fraud and phishing emails

NEVER trust strange looking emails that say they need more information; they're from identity thieves who are trying to nab your social security number and credit card information.

If it looks real, *close the email*, log into your eBay or PayPal account and check for messages *within your account*. Maybe a credit card has expired.

If you have ANY doubt that an email message is from eBay, forward it to spoof@ebay.com immediately. Same goes for PayPal – report to spoof@paypal.com.

When you forward, DO NOT remove the original subject line or change the email in any way.

WHAT TO SELL

If it's interesting, desirable and easy to ship, it's probably right for eBay. I prefer vintage jewelry because it's so portable.

If you've inherited an entire estate from a parent or relative, the work begins. (I talk about selling large items in Chapter 16.) Check house, attic, basement, yard, garage and storage buildings for antique or vintage:

Advertising memorabilia, ads and signs
Appliances and stoves
Automotive parts, accessories and manuals
Beer/alcohol signs and ads
Bedding, linens, spreads, chenille and embroidered items
Bird houses
Boating miscellany, from boat parts to ads
Books of all kinds
Bottles
Cameras
China and dinnerware
Clocks
Clothing and shoes
Coins and paper money
Dolls, dollhouses and accessories
Drapes
Fabrics
Fashion-related items, including purses, hats, compacts and sewing patterns
Figurines and planters
Fishing poles, lures and related
Folk art
Furniture – indoor and outdoor
Games and playing cards
Garden décor, tools and implements
Glass, art glass, vases, glasses and pitchers
Globes and maps, framed and otherwise

Gold *anything*
Historical items, from books, letters and medals to magazines
Holiday jewelry and decorations
Hunting decoys and collectibles
Jewelry, ring settings, watches and pocket watches
Kitchen stuff; cookbooks, cookware, bowls, dishes and silverware
Lamps, lighting and fixtures – oil or electrified – floor, hanging, or wall
Letters and photographs
Luggage, suitcases; overnight, cosmetic and hat bags
Magazines
Medals, pins and badges
Military memorabilia of any type, from letters to uniforms
Movie, music and celebrity memorabilia
Musical instruments – harmonicas, guitars, violins, etc.
Native American jewelry, beadwork, etc.
Office chairs, typewriters, etc.
Pens, inkwells and writing accessories
Pictures, paintings, mirrors and frames
Porcelain and pottery
Postcards, posters and prints
Radios, record players and vinyl records
Religious/spiritual medals and remembrances
Rugs and textiles
Sewing machines and accessories
Silver and silver-plate trays, candlesticks and more
Sports memorabilia, cards and autographs
Telephones
Tobacco collectibles
Tools and hardware
Toys, mechanical and otherwise – model cars, model trains, etc.
Transportation – cars, motorcycles, tractors, etc.
Trunks

WHEN TO SELL

While birthdays, anniversaries and guilt gifting occur all year long, I pay special attention to seasons and holidays.

In fall I sell jewelry in autumn colors; brown, rust and purple add depth and beauty to sweaters, jackets and coats.

(Art nouveau brooch with amethyst glass on goldtone)

The third Saturday of October brings Sweetest Day. This silly butterfly is an incredibly vibrant, sparkling red. It's also out of whack.

(My whimsical, fabulously flawed butterfly)

I took it out for Sweetest Day; but found I couldn't part with it.

32

I watch for jewelry with a creepy Goth vibe all year long and list it before Halloween.

I found this bracelet in a resale shop; the beads are lampwork. It was previously owned, but I don't know if it had been worn. I list items like this "estate" rather than "vintage."

(Great glossy beads with skulls, spiders and webs)

November and December are my best months.

(Vintage Taxco silver bells; right for the season)

List your finest for Christmas.

While customers may buy vintage jewelry any time of the year, they seem to pay more per item before major holidays.

(The real thing: diamonds in 14k gold)

January is a mixed bag as consumers deal with the awful truth of their post-holiday credit card statements; although those who received money as gifts may still be looking to spend it.

February gives us the hearts, hugs and kisses of Valentine's Day.

(Hearts & keys are perfect for Valentine's Day.)

I remind the single ladies there's nothing wrong with treating yourself to something special!

In early spring – when the first crocus is peeking up through the last of the winter snows – I sell my most colorful jewelry and shell themes.

(Goldtone shell bracelet marked Germany)

Keep it going!

Adornments related to religion, history and ancestry are desirable *year-round.* This medal was purchased by a fashion designer in Italy. I was flattered when he invited me to friend him on Facebook.

(Marie Antoinette pendant, sold 2013)

WHO TO SELL

Every time I list an item, I imagine who might buy.

When you sell on eBay, you're selling to moms and dads, single parents with kids, teenagers/young adults, gay and straight, active or retired military, grandmothers and grandfathers on fixed incomes.

You are selling to people who are squeaking to get by and people who *have it made*; they're watching and ready to spend.

When you sell estate jewelry you're selling to people who are:

- Purchasing to wear
- Adding to their collections
- Buying gifts for others
- Purchasing to resell online or off

If you're selling what you love, your target market is people like you.

We're not in Kansas any more

If you have a small town mindset, lose it; eBay is a global marketplace with separate sites in 25 countries. About 30% of my best jewelry goes overseas; and some styles that don't sell well here are popular abroad.

When I was down with Lyme, the international aspect of online transactions expanded my limited horizons.

Customer service will make or break you

Honor them with honest, thorough listings, painstaking packaging and positive feedback. That's right, if there's a problem, resolve it and try to leave everything on good terms.

(Fingers crossed, I've never had an issue.)

CHAPTER 4: TOOLS & SUPPLIES

You don't know what it's worth until you know what it is.

I spent about $100 (total) for a loupe, gold test kit, jewelry scale, diamond tester and ring sizer. We need to try to identify:

- Type of metal
- Weight in grams (for gold and silver)
- Manufacturer or designer
- Size/dimensions
- Condition
- Age/period/style

These simple tools have helped me identify, price and sell *thousands* in jewelry.

Jeweler's loupe – $20 & up

I chose a 10x True Professional Quality loupe with a triplet lens. I use it to find designer marks, hallmarks, gold marks, silver marks, etc.

- Rings are usually marked inside the band
- Earrings are usually marked on the post or back
- Necklaces and chains are usually marked on the clasp

When you're trying to identify a piece, don't limit your search to the obvious locations; many significant marks are hidden in the nooks and crannies. This is especially true with earrings and bracelets.

Ring sizing stick – $5 & up

ALWAYS include ring size in title and description. Unless the piece is spectacular, people do not want to gamble on size or pay a jeweler to make it fit.

Gold test kit – $20 or less

If the piece isn't marked – but you suspect it may be valuable – test for it. A full gold test kit will allow you to determine if a metal is 10k, 14k, 18k or 22k gold – or silver or platinum. Follow the directions and be careful – it's acid, after all!

Digital jewelry scale – $8 & up

Buyers want to know the actual weight of silver, gold or platinum jewelry. I use a digital pocket scale and post the grams in the title – as in "14k Italy bracelet, 31 grams." It's an easy way for savvy customers to compare *your* price per gram vs. the competition.

And yes, go ahead and take a photo of the item on the scale; I just don't recommend using it as the main photo.

Diamond tester – $20 & up

I bought a Dusiec™ Jewelry Diamond Tester Selector II Gems Gemstone Tester LED Tool. It offered low price and ease of use.

Read the directions carefully. Before purchasing the tester, I guessed the stones flanking a peridot ring were faux because the band wasn't marked. I nearly put it out to auction at a low price.

Testing showed the stones were real!

Jewelry polishing cloth – about $10

I recommend a two-piece polishing cloth that's designed to clean and buff silver and gold; something like Hagerty Polishing Cloths.

Jewelry cleaner with cleaning basket and brush – about $10

Read the directions before you dunk. The ammoniated versions are good for hard gems, but they'll dissolve pearls and porous stones.

Small zip-lock plastic bags – about $6.00

Most metal will tarnish when exposed to air; especially silver. I keep all of my better jewelry in Cousin Bagettes. (They come in jewelry-friendly sizes.)

When my items sell, I ship them in the bag in a gift box.

Jewelry making tool kit for repairs – about $20

My kit includes:

- Needle nose pliers
- Flat nose pliers
- Round nose pliers
- Cutter
- Calipers

A magnifying glass and felt beading tray come in handy as well.

More on simple repairs in Chapter 8

Shipping supplies

Much of what we need is free.

- Small and medium boxes, usually recycled
- Paper grocery bags to cover recycled boxes
- Priority Mail Small Flat Rate boxes; free from usps.com
- Adhesive tape/packaging tape
- Padded envelopes
- Gift boxes or clean cardboard to create protective boxes
- Bubble wrap or tissue

More on shipping supplies in Chapter 12

CHAPTER 5: EXAMINING YOUR JEWELRY

The old pin with purple glass might be an art nouveau brooch with amethyst glass. The goldtone bracelet *(?)* with the strange clasp might be a 100 year old 9k gold *watch* chain. The coin pendant with foreign writing could be a historic medal.

How do you determine what's what?

The best way to assess (and later describe) is to search eBay for similar pieces. Always choose Vintage Jewelry and include Title and Description under Advanced Search.

This is how eBay breaks it down.

Fine jewelry

eBay categories for fine vintage jewelry include:

- Charm & Charm Bracelets
- Georgian, pre-1837
- Victorian and Edwardian, 1837 to 1910
- Art Nouveau and Art Deco, 1895-1935
- Retro and vintage, 1930s to 1980s
- Designer/Signed
- Men's Vintage Fine Jewelry
- Unknown Period
- Other

Materials for fine vintage jewelry include gold, gold-filled, platinum, silver and combinations with or without stones.

Costume jewelry

Make no mistake, stellar costume jewelry can sell for as much – or more than – ordinary gold or silver jewelry.

40

eBay categories for costume vintage jewelry include:

- Georgian, pre-1837
- Victorian and Edwardian, 1837 to 1910
- Art Nouveau and Art Deco, 1895-1935
- Retro and vintage, 1930s to 1980s
- Bakelite and Vintage Plastics
- Designer/Signed
- Men's Vintage Costume Jewelry
- Unknown Period
- Other

Materials for the vintage category include rhinestone, gold-plate, goldtone, silver-plate, silvertone, gems, stones, simulants and glass.

Jewelry dating basics

Pins and brooches

If the pin is longer than the brooch, it's mid-1800s.

C-clasps (like the one on this rocking horse) are 1900s and earlier.

Safety clasps (with swivel mechanisms) were patented in 1901 and continue to be used.

Some of the better brooches have loops so they can also be worn as pendants.

(This versatile brooch could also be worn as a pendant.)

Dress clips – a.k.a. fur clips (with hinged clasps) were popular from the 1930s to the 1950s.

Pierced earrings

Pierced earrings have been around for thousands of years and they were worn by women *and* men. Pirates wore them to commemorate epic passages, like crossing the equator or surviving Cape Horn.

(From Wikipedia: Capture of the Pirate Blackbeard, 1718)

They believed silver and gold had mystical properties that could protect vision and hearing or prevent them from drowning.

Being a pirate was risky business; they had good reason to fear they might be buried in a foreign land or dumped at sea. Livescience.com tells us some engraved the name of their home ports inside their earrings so their bodies could be shipped home for burial.

It's not likely we'll encounter ancient artifacts, but we do run across items from the 1800s & 1900s.

Screwback earrings date from 1894 to the mid-1950s. They can be a tough sell.

(Old screwbacks with lovely red rhinestones)

Clip earrings were patented in 1934; they were most popular in the 1950s and 1960s.

In the 80s it was fashionable to wear *monstrous* clip earrings like Linda Evans and Joan Collins on Dynasty. Despite the padded backs on the better styles, they numbed your lobes and had to be removed to prevent unholy clanking on the phone.

Some manufacturers continue to make clip earrings today.

Omega backs were introduced in the 70s. They're easy to wear and *very* secure.

(Omega backs on emerald earrings I sold in 2012)

Necklace and bracelet clasps

- Fold-over clasps were introduced in the 40s and can still be found today.
- Hook clasps (that attach to one of the last beads on a strand or last loops on a chain) were most common in the 50s and 60s.
- Box clasps are usually pre-1950; they usually match the necklace (often beaded) and closure involves insertion of a tab.
- Spring clasps have been around for decades.
- Barrel clasps were fairly common in the 1970s and 80s; they are *hell* on long hair.
- Lobster clasps and toggle clasps (a bar slipped into a circle) are modern/newer.

Multi-layered beaded necklaces – as well as those with aurora borealis stones – are usually 1950s.

As a small child, their beauty made long hours in the Kingdom Hall a little less miserable.

(Five glorious strands of pinks and purples with art glass)

Designer/manufacturer marks and hallmarks

A manufacturer's name and associated facts yield far better profits than a listing without identification and details.

When you find initials, do a Google search to determine if they're significant. Every time you do a Google search, it goes through all the sale sites – including Ruby Lane, Etsy and others. It also picks up information from collectors who blog.

True Story: The Amethyst Glass Brooch

I've had some pieces elude identification for years. I was polishing an antique brooch with amethyst glass when I noticed a mark on the c-clasp.

I had to dig out my loupe to read it – "G.L.P." I did a Google search for "antique jewelry GLP." The best results came from a blog, Pink Astilbe Vintage Jewelry: www.rebelmouse.com/PinkAstilbe/

She had researched G.L.P. and found it stood for George L. Paine Company in Massachusetts.

He was in business in the late 1800s, early 1900s and had a reputation for producing gold and gold-filled jewelry.

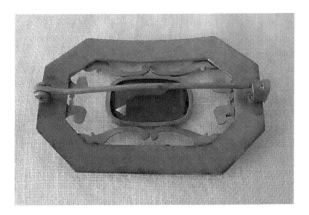

(Brass c-clasp brooch/sash pin with amethyst glass)

Smart lady – the blogger included a link to a G.L.P. amethyst glass brooch in her Etsy store.

She also has a Facebook presence; *way to go!*

I did more searches on eBay and found brooches similar to mine priced from $35 to $95.

Spend time at the Antique Jewelry University

It's one of the most comprehensive online reference sites I've found. It covers everything from the history of jewelry by period (from ancient to American) to jewelry hallmarks, manufacture, gemology, gems and more.

Explore www.antiquejewelryuniversity.com

When an item evades identification

Don't assume it's insignificant. Put it away until you have more information.

CHAPTER 6: IDENTIFYING METALS

Silver Jewelry

Silver may be marked silver, sterling, sterling silver, argent, argent sterling, 925, 92.5, .925.

(A silver ring, easily identified)

Jewelry marked 900 is 900/1000 parts silver. Mexican silver marks include 980, 960, 940, 925, 900 and more. Note that location codes matter too! (Taxco is a favorite.)

See the Online Encyclopedia of Silver Marks, Hallmarks & Makers' Marks, including American, British, Mexican, Irish, and Russian marks: www.925-1000.com

HSE is heavy silver electroplate.

Gold Jewelry

Gold is usually marked 10k, 14k, 18k, or 22k. If your item is followed by a "p" – as in *14kp* – that means "plumb" or "exactly" 14k.

European marks reflect the percentage of pure gold content, as in:

- 8k gold = 333 (33.3%)
- 9k gold = 375 (37.5%)
- 10k gold = 416 (41.6%)
- 12k gold = 500 (50%)
- 14k gold = 585 (58.5%)
- 18k gold = 750 (75%)
- 20k gold = 833 (83.3%)
- 21k gold = 875 (87.5%)
- 22k gold = 917 (91.7%)

Gold plated and gold filled items are marked:

- GE – gold electroplate
- HGE – heavy gold electroplate
- RGP – rolled gold plate
- GF – gold filled

(18k HGE ring with tiger's eye stone)

"1/20 10k G.F." means the piece has 1/20th of its total weight in 10 karat gold. (Use the same reasoning for 1/10, 1/20 and 1/30 of *whatever* karat gold filled.)

Original condition – *or not*

Some buyers want the item to be 100% original – patina & all; the decision is yours. To me, it depends on the piece.

I bought a lot of antique Buddhist pendants from Thailand; some of the brass amulets were so dark with age you could barely make out the figures. *Light* hand buffing with a polishing cloth brought them to life. I kept the best and sold the rest.

About pendants and chains

I believe in selling jewelry that's ready to wear. It's acceptable to sell a good gold pendant without a chain – or a good gold chain without a pendant. But it's best to sell *sets* when you're selling lesser metals.

You can usually find old chains cheap at resale shops. Once you have a nice selection, it's easy to pair a lone pendant with the right chain; simply match metals and proportions as best you can.

(Vintage Thai amulet on a repurposed chain)

If your pendant or medal has lost its bail, you can find connectors, bails and jump rings in a variety of metals on eBay under Beads & Jewelry Making.

CHAPTER 7: PRICING GOLD & FINE JEWELRY

You can't Google "how to sell gold jewelry" without being bombarded with ads from gold buying sites.

DO NOT see them in person – as I did – or send your valuables through the mail expecting fair payment. Please DO Google the horror stories of those who have.

Common sense tells us they can't make money paying us what gold is truly worth; we have to sell it ourselves.

How to sell gold jewelry

This is my actual process.

I wanted to sell 14k gold earrings that weighed 8.9 grams. They were marked "Italy" and featured deep green enamel.

My ex bought them for me because he thought they were gorgeous. I didn't like them; I wore them a few times to be polite.

(They looked better in color; 14k gold earrings with green enamel)

I didn't know how to describe the closure, so I did a search of premium gold earrings. I learned they're called "Omega" posts or backs, an important feature.

Gold prices vary daily, so I went to goldprice.org and (that day) the price was $1,609.78.

To determine price per gram, I divided by 31.1 (the troy ounce measurement for precious metals) to arrive at a price of $51.76 per gram.

Note that this price is for gold that's 99.5% fine; 14k gold is 58.3% pure gold; 22k is 92%, 18k is 75%, 10k is 41% and 9k is 38%.

I calculated as follows:

$51.76 x .583 = $30.17 per gram for 14k gold

$30.17 per gram x 8.9 grams = $268.57

That became my bottom line. I would not sell for less.

It didn't seem like enough, so I searched eBay's Completed Listings; click Advanced (near the Search bar) to find this section.

The prices for enamel jewelry were stupid low, so I searched "14k Italy;" those earrings were selling for about $45.00 per gram. That's more like it!

I listed the earrings for $400 – $45 per gram – under Buy it Now with Best Offer.

It's better to list high and lower the price than live with the knowledge that you settled for less.

I listed as follows ...

Estate 1980s ITALY GREEN ENAMEL 14k Yellow Gold Omega Post Earrings 8.9 Grams

"My husband bought these for me many years ago; he thought I looked great in green. They're nearly 1 ¼" long x ½" wide and weigh 8.9 grams.

14k Italy is clearly marked as shown – the color of the gold is exceptional and the Omega backs are very comfortable.

(I am also listing another pair I no longer wear.)

Exactly as shown, no returns."

I received (and happily accepted) a Best Offer that was only 10% less than my listed price. I'm guessing I would have received about $60 from the gold buyers.

QUICK REVIEW

When selling fine jewelry …

- Establish actual value by checking the gold price for that day.
- Calculate as described.
- Arrive at a real-world jewelry value by reviewing Completed Listings.
- Be absolutely accurate about condition; with estate jewelry, some wear is acceptable.
- Remember that style is part of the value; in this case, the green enamel I disliked was highly prized by my buyer.

If your item doesn't attract watchers or receive offers, you can always end the listing and relist before the holidays.

The green enamel earrings were purchased by a buyer in the U.S. Virgin Islands. Shipping was easy peasy.

Pricing silver

Calculations, weight and values haven't worked for me here; origin (location), style, maker and stones have been everything.

To get your best price on silver, do painstaking research. I like The Online Encyclopedia of Silver Marks, Hallmarks & Makers' Marks: www.925-1000.com

In most cases it takes a gemologist to distinguish lab created diamond and emerald knockoffs from genuine precious stones; but in the case of turquoise, malachite, agate and the like, it just takes a good eye.

Begin by searching the web and eBay by color of stone.

Once you have details, Completed Listings will give you an idea of how much you can charge.

If you suspect the item is something special

Consider having your item professionally appraised. It's easier to sell jewelry when you have a new – or even an older – appraisal.

Here in Fort Myers I'm told I can get appraisals from $50 to $100 per piece.

Pricing gold filled, gold electroplate, etc.

Scrutinize the piece for initials/hallmarks and price based on what you find in Completed Listings.

Remember; style is a factor with *any* metal.

Keep your notes!

They save time when you list, relist or sell something similar. I save my notes to Word files in "old" and "live" eBay folders.

CHAPTER 8: MANAGING CONDITION ISSUES

When faced with a troubling condition issue, consult Google or YouTube.

In Chapter 5 I wrote about the amethyst glass brooch marked GLP; I failed to mention there was a serious tarnish issue. I googled "how to remove tarnish on brass."

The solution was as close as the fridge. I learned ketchup will eat tarnish; who knew? I applied it with a cotton swab and left it on for about 30 minutes; then I rinsed and buffed. When I was done, the brooch was worth twice its pre-condiment value.

Missing rhinestones

If you can match the size and color you can (sometimes) fix it yourself. This is why it's smart to keep broken pieces, one earring from a set, etc.

Search YouTube for tutorials on repair methods, from "how to fix a broken jewelry clasp" to "how to glue rhinestones."

If you don't have stray elements that fit, the better bead stores can be a great resource; take the piece with you.

Those of us who aren't blessed with proximity have to wing it online. For instance, if you need rhinestones, search eBay as follows:

Jewelry & Watches – Loose Beads – Rhinestones *or* Jewelry & Watches – Vintage & Antique Jewelry – Costume – Retro, Vintage 1930s-1980s – Collections, Lots

Bungled bracelets

Buyers don't want to see unruly baubles replete with clumps, clusters and gaps.

Spread the bracelet out perfectly flat and consider the balance in terms of size and color. In most cases charms are easy to rearrange. (Be extremely gentle bending old links as they may break.)

When I find empty links, I remove them. They tell the buyer "something is missing." (Save empty links for future repairs.) Work around (or cut/remove) soldered links.

True Story: **The Order of the Garter Bracelet**

The last bracelet I worked with had soldered links – but one of the charms had broken off; it was unsellable, a smile without a front tooth. I was ready to stuff it in a drawer for parts when research showed the smallest charm (lower left) commemorates the ancient Order of the Garter. (It pays to be a history geek; I won't bore you with details.)

I went through my collection of antique medals and found a charm that seemed appropriate in terms of chivalric theme and size.

(I replaced the missing link with St. Anne de Beaupre.)

When I listed, I explained the Order of the Garter, described how I replaced the missing link with St. Anne de Beaupre, explained who she was and emphasized that she has value and significance all her own.

If the bracelet is good but the charms are cheap, consider removing the charms and selling the bracelet by itself. Likewise, if the charms are worthy but the bracelet is inconsequential, consider selling the charms separately.

Seeking expert assistance

If you need real stones – or the repair is beyond your abilities – find a good jeweler who charges fair rates. I found mine at a local pawn shop. He's horribly fussy, with an eye for detail and access to a variety of stones in unusual sizes.

I'm confident selling anything he fixes and usually add "inspected by a professional jeweler" to my descriptions.

True Story: The Gold Garnet Ring

I had a petite 14k gold ring with a marquis shaped garnet. It looked fine – until I viewed it through my loupe.

(14k gold ring with marquis shaped garnet)

The prongs on either side of the stone were empty; I believe they originally held seed pearls. I was tempted to sell as-is, but I knew I wouldn't get what the ring was truly worth.

My jeweler didn't have seed pearls, but he did have tiny garnets that matched the stone perfectly. *He only charged $25!*

The ring sold quickly in Buy it Now with Best Offer; I made a nice profit and the buyer was pleased.

When the stone is bad

Have a less than perfect ring? That's ok; you can sell the setting with or without the stone. (I've seen them described as "Scrap or Wear.")

If you're selling *with*, be honest about the condition of the stone while emphasizing the beauty and value of the vintage setting. Some buyers are happy to enjoy the ring as is.

Selling as-is

I don't bother with repairs if the cost will consume my potential for profit.

True Story: The Bohemian Garnet Ring

My jeweler couldn't find antique Bohemian garnets to match this ring and he didn't know of any other sources.

(Bohemian garnet ring with missing stones)

I listed as-is, drew attention to the two missing stones and priced it fairly in Buy it Now with Best Offer.

It had many watchers for a long time. The day after Valentine's Day it sold at full price, *without* negotiation.

Sometimes all you need is patience.

Don't throw anything out!

It's a hoarder's mantra, but it's true. Jewelry that's not fit for sale can be valuable for parts – links, charms, chains, rhinestones, clasps and more.

During your online searches and real world travels, watch for broken or discounted jewelry with old garnets and other stones that could come in handy as spares.

LEARNING SIMPLE REPAIR SKILLS

If you want to specialize in estate jewelry, I urge you to take a jewelry making class. You'll learn to wire wrap, bead, create closures and more.

I have used basic jewelry-making skills to:

- Lengthen antique necklaces and bracelets that were too short for modern necks and wrists.
- Restring beaded necklaces.
- Create custom silver bails.
- Replace broken clasps.
- Secure old connectors; very often the metal only needs a simple adjustment to close properly.
- Create earrings, bracelets and necklaces from antique crystals and beads.
- Replace ugly, corroded or uncomfortable earwires.
- Remove or attach charms and medals from/to vintage bracelets.

Sometimes I convert screwback earrings to earwires; they're far more comfortable. (Research the original value before you do this.) I consider zeelver.com the best wholesale resource for high quality Bali and Thai silver and gold-filled earwires and findings.

Buy a jewelry making tool kit

Whether you take a class or not, it's worth your while to have a tool kit. They're about $20 in the crafts areas of eBay, Michael's or your favorite store. My kit includes needle nose pliers, flat nose pliers, round nose pliers, a cutter and calipers.

A felt beading tray comes in handy for keeping beads, findings and tools in place as you work.

CHAPTER 9: WRITING DESCRIPTIONS

Better descriptions yield higher profits.

Prepare your description immediately after the identification process, while the details are fresh in your mind. I create mine in a Word document so I can copy and paste to eBay; I save the file in case the item doesn't sell and I decide to relist later.

I usually create my descriptions from scratch, but you can take cues from a similar listing. *(See Chapter 11: Listing Your Items)*

Potential buyers want to know:

- Cut/type of stones (i.e. marquis cut garnet, pear shaped topaz, oval amethyst, emerald cut peridot)
- Color of stones or glass
- Type/color of metal (i.e. 14k yellow gold)
- Weight of silver, gold or platinum
- Manufacturer or designer initials/name
- Sizes – as in how big the stone, how long/wide the chain, etc.; always measure antique necklaces and bracelets as ladies were much smaller 100 years ago
- The age, style or period of the piece
- Condition – usually it's appropriate for the item's age
- Accessories – if an antique ring or bracelet comes with its original box, say so. It usually adds to the value. In some cases, the box can be worth more than the jewelry.

If you don't know the difference between styles, as in don't know your deco from your nouveau – simply mention both; something like "Lovely deco or nouveau piece with ...."

It seems to me newbies care most that the piece is vintage; while discriminating collectors know the facts at a glance.

You just need to help them find your listing.

(Is this nouveau? It's ok to say you don't know.)

If you *think* it's an unmarked designer piece, mention the possible designers and manufacturers.

Use every appropriate search word, just avoid presenting your suspicions as fact.

Do remember that wishful thinking and accidental deception can come back to bite in the form of negative feedback. When I started buying in '98, people were trying to pass HGE off as gold.

No, it's not gold – it's heavy gold electroplate. *Nice try.*

Selling unmarked metals

When you've tested an item, be sure to say "unmarked but tests as...." Sometimes I assume silver based on style and stone; as in Native American jewelry.

When in doubt, I price low and/or guarantee the item.

Embracing the obvious

She has helmet hair, a linebacker's neck and no discernible jawline.

I sold this cameo by suggesting she might make a suitable gift for frenemy or mother-in-law.

Selling charm bracelets

It's easy to sell bracelets. *Nobody* says "I hate my wrists!" Over the years lobes may droop, necks may wrinkle and fingers may gnarl ... but wrists remain pretty much the same.

As I write I'm wearing a $9.99 purchase with a comical dragon, a fat brass Buddha and assorted goofiness. It feels light on my wrist and it makes me happy.

If your bracelet is 7" or less, that's fairly small. You might add "extenders can be purchased on eBay" to your description.

When working with silver and combination bracelets, examine every charm carefully; your prospect wants to know which elements are silver and which aren't.

Mention every *type* of charm. The budding ballerina will find your bracelet because you listed toe shoes!

People like to skim, so I list types of charms in caps, as follows:

Vintage SILVER CHARM BRACELET Bible Lord's Prayer Sports Mechanicals 28.8 g

Vintage 1944 sports themed silver charm bracelet w mechanical elements. 7 charms: Bible, Lord's Prayer, Mermaid, Pennant, Basketball, Bullhorn, Pic frame

ALL ORIGINAL: Nothing added, nothing removed

This 67 year old bracelet features:

- Red and blue PENNANT marked sterling
- A lovely Christian Catholic BIBLE with a cross on front; it opens to reveal full Lord's Prayer
- A square with flowers engraved "N.E.S. 6-25-44"
- Cheerleading BULLHORN marked sterling
- A hollow BASKETBALL that opens to reveal a secret compartment
- A GRADUATION DAY book with cap and diploma on cover and two picture holders inside

- A smiling topless MERMAID holding a shell to her ear, beautiful detail front and rear.

PLEASE NOTE! The end of her tail is missing. If this bothers you, I would simply remove or replace.

Sterling stamps are on links or charms; I couldn't find Sterling notation on the basketball, it may be on the inside.

7.5" Inches long
Total Weight: 28.8 grams"

Note all the search words! That's how your item gets found.

Selling religious bracelets

I'm not Catholic, but I admire expressions of faith.

If it's a bracelet with religious medals, consider listing all saints and popes, with a quick description of each. (Where they were born, what they were famous for, etc.)

Some medals are revered for protective properties; write about them. For example, St. Christopher is the patron saint of travelers and Saint Francis of Assisi is the patron saint of animals.

There are many Catholic resources online. Try Catholic.org, AmericanCatholic.org and Catholic-saints.info – or just do a Google search.

Adding this type of information to your descriptions attracts religious and spiritually inclined individuals, adding meaning and significance to your offerings.

Keeping collections intact

When I buy religious medals and collections from estates, I like to keep them together.

I have an entire collection from one individual in my "to do" box. It's more than medals. When I find the right silver bracelet, I will attach the prettiest medals. When it sells I'll include *everything* that came with it.

And yes, I believe some objects retain the spiritual essence of the person who wore them. One of my Catholic bracelets makes me feel safe, as if I'm protected by an army of angels.

I would have liked to have known the previous owner.

Promoting birthstones

Birthstone jewelry is a popular gift year-round, perfect for holidays and anniversaries as well.

Many people search for birthstone jewelry by month, so add it to your description; as in "Garnet ring, *birthstone for January.*"

- January: Garnet
- February: Amethyst
- March: Aquamarine
- April: Diamond
- May: Emerald
- June: Pearl or Alexandrite
- July: Ruby
- August: Peridot
- September: Sapphire
- October: Tourmaline or Opal
- November: Topaz or Citrine
- December: Tanzanite, Zircon or Turquoise

Some people can't afford the real thing.

If you're selling estate jewelry with colored glass or rhinestones that match a certain birthstone, you can use the *color* in the description, as in "peridot green."

The prongs on this birthstone ring worried me, so I took it to my jeweler. He said he doesn't like to work with gold this old, it can break; but I had his reassurance the stone is solid in the setting.

I documented the interaction in my description.

(An old emerald cut peridot birthstone in 10k yellow gold)

Featuring metaphysical properties

If it's a very special item, I research the spiritual qualities of the stone and add them to the description. For instance, amethysts are considered to have healing properties. Rose quartz is said to ease physical and emotional issues.

Simply believing can be a comfort.

TELLING STORIES THAT SELL

Stories help prospects form emotional connections with your items based on person, place or time.

Who is it from?

I'm drawn to items that are part of an estate, from sellers who are listing jewelry handed down by family members. When you see listings like these, always check the seller's other items.

True Story: The Givré Beads

Years ago I bought a small collection of necklaces and bracelets with peach givré beads. (Givré is French for frost. Givré beads feature transparent glass around a translucent center.)

The yellowed price tags were still attached to the jewelry and the boxes were from one of Detroit's better department stores. The seller told me her aunt bought them, stored them and never wore them.

She waited all her life for an occasion that never came.

I displayed them in my shop. One woman was deeply moved when I told her about the original owner. She bought them and promised they *would* be worn.

Where is it from?

Place has the power to transport, if only through imagination.

In southeast Michigan, much of my merchandise came from estate and garage sales in waterfront towns that have been vacation destinations for generations.

I've easily sold jewelry I purchased in Italy, Aspen and Playa del Carmen (near Cozumel) fifteen to twenty years ago.

I explain the Mexican purchases were fueled by too many margaritas, which gives me an opportunity to amuse the cocktail demographic.

(Enormous Taxco silver shell pendant)

When is it from?

The time period can speak volumes.

True Story: The WWII Bracelet with Aviator Charms

One summer I snagged an old silver bracelet with unusual Italian charms for very little money. The most interesting charm was a functioning bell with "Capri" & "Campanina Della Fortuna San Michele" on the front and a four leaf clover on the back.

Research led me to Barbi Ennis Connolly's collection of aviator jackets on 57thbombwing.com.

The bell had ties to the ancient miracle of a poor shepherd boy who was reunited with his beloved lost sheep through divine intervention.

The site explained that the four leaf clover on the back of the bell featured one leaf for fame, one for wealth, one for faithful love and one for glorious health.

WWII aviators considered the bell good luck and wore it on their flight jackets.

This bell wound up on a wife or girlfriend's bracelet – along with other unique charms, including a mechanical globe that opened to reveal tiny photos of Spanish bullfights.

Yet another charm was an Italian fist or "figa" – an obscenity.

(The figa – or fist – is upper left)

And there were glorious Etruscan fobs with colorful cabochons.

(One of the fobs; both had compartments)

The thing was incredible, a weighty memento of WWII, a celebration of The Greatest Generation. I painstakingly researched and described. It took time, but I enjoy that sort of thing.

The buyer thanked me for my efforts. She was pleased to possess an heirloom with details.

HISTORY & ANCESTRY THAT SELL

Imagine what this country has experienced in the past 200 years: the Underground Railroad, the Civil War, the *(first)* Great Depression and two world wars.

American families have *so much history*. And eBay feeds our need to collect the tangibles with categories that include antiquities, books, manuscripts, maps, maritime, science, medicine and more.

How have the past two centuries affected *your* family?

I recently learned my great grandfather left his wife and their small son (my grandfather) during the depression; he hopped a train and headed west to "visit his mother."

My great grandmother received a few letters but *he never came back*; he simply started a *new* family!

How long did it take him to get out west? Was he a hobo during that time? I know he was an artist. Despite – *or because of* – the sad family story, I'm suddenly drawn to tramp art; it was made by hobos and untrained artists from the period after the Civil War through the Great Depression.

My friend Patte – an antique dealer – collects *trench* art made from shell casings. Wikipedia describes it as "any decorative item made by soldiers, prisoners of war or civilians, where the manufacture is directly linked to armed conflict or its consequences."

Genealogy Geeks

How many amateur genealogists are there? As of September, 2012, Ancestry.com had 2 million paying subscribers – including me.

Passion for genealogy naturally transitions to obsession with the history of your ancestor's place and period in time.

Years ago my mother hired a genealogist. I expected her research would yield bootleggers and whores. You can imagine my surprise when she learned we are descendants of Sir Thomas Wyatt the Poet.

There are probably thousands of us in the U.S.

I'm in the process of writing a book on the Tudor era Wyatts. Sir Henry Wyatt served Henry VII, Sir Thomas Wyatt the Poet served Henry VIII and Sir Thomas Wyatt the Younger led an unsuccessful rebellion against Queen Mary and died a traitor's death.

My blog is www.sirthomaswyattthepoet.com I use Ancestry.com and historical sources to explore the branches; and eBay searches lead me to obscure books and publications!

I've learned you can frequently find the same books at lower prices on Amazon. If the book is very old, it may be available to read for free in PDF or other formats.

True Story: Epiphany at Edinburgh Castle

Remember my strange experience in Edinburgh Castle? I was never quite sure what that was. I assumed I was overcome by antiquity.

In 2012 I went on ancestry.com and traced my Grandpa Bolen's line back to Margaret of Wessex – a.k.a. Queen Margaret of Scotland – SAINT Margaret. She was born in 1045 and died in 1093.

Saint Margaret is my 29th Great Grandmother through my Bolen line! We connect again through the Wyatt line. It was 3 a.m., but time was irrelevant; I had been transported a thousand years.

Each day Margaret served the needs of orphans and the poor before feeding herself. Shakespeare wrote that she spent more time on her knees than her feet.

A life of austerity and fasting took their toll on her health.

After learning her husband and son had been killed in battle against the English, *she took her last breath in Edinburgh Castle.*

The moment I read that I experienced the *exact other-worldly sensation* I had within those stone walls as a kid; my flesh crawled, from my scalp to my fingertips.

(Wikipedia – St. Margaret's Chapel at Edinburgh Castle; photo by Jonathan Oldenbuck)

The following morning I went on eBay hoping to find a religious medal in her honor. I saved the search. In time a vintage silver Saint Margaret medal came through and I will *never* sell it.

Many descendants and history buffs experience this profound sense of connection.

Keepers of the memories

Some of us want to see these objects "go home." One of my ongoing searches is for "coin" because people don't know how to describe historic medals.

It annoys me to find improperly described medals and historically significant items in the jewelry section.

If a "pendant" has words, some of us feel the need to find out what they're all about.

True Story: The Daughter of Marie Antoinette

One day a large medal appeared in one of my automated searches. The seller described the piece as "LARGE Antique Silvertone COIN Relic Pendant 24" Necklace."

(Marie Therese Duchesse D'Angouleme, daughter of Marie Antoinette and King Louis XVI)

I clicked to learn more: under magnification, one side of the medal showed an elegant young woman with her hair up in curls; she was a mature woman on the other side.

I remembered seeing this young/old format with Queen Victoria's coins. She was intriguing and I remembered enough French to realize she was significant.

In the last 10 seconds I slammed a maximum of $27.00 and won the piece for $13.84 plus $2.95 shipping.

Once I had the medal in my hot little hands, I could examine the wording with my loupe. She was Marie Therese Duchesse D'Angouleme, daughter of Marie Antoinette and King Louis XVI.

"Marie-Thérèse de France" survived the French Revolution and married her cousin Louis-Antoine, duc d'Angoulême.

When I listed, I wrote the medal was "obviously a historical piece that needs to be in the hands of a descendant/relative or appreciative collector."

I found an article and quoted much of it. Marie Therese spent much of her childhood imprisoned alone in the Tower of the Temple. Before Napoleon razed the building in 1811, there, "scratched upon the wall of the room where the child, Marie-Thérèse, lived her solitary life, these piteous words:

'Marie-Thérèse is the most unhappy creature in the world. She can obtain no news of her mother; nor be reunited to her, though she has asked it a thousand times.'

'Live, my good mother! whom I love well, but of whom I can hear no tidings.'

'O my father! watch over me from heaven above.'

'O my God! forgive those who have made my family die.'"

eBay does not allow us to include links, the best I could do was name the source. (Penn Libraries, http://digital.library.upenn.edu)

I put her out to auction with a starting price of $45 and that's what she sold for.

I hoped Marie Therese would be found by a relative or descendant; I never dreamed she would find her way home. I carefully packed her in a pretty blue box and shipped her back to France.

The buyer's feedback made me smile: "médaille très originale – envoi parfait – A RECOMMANDER +++++++++++++"

FASHIONS THAT SELL

Which cable series and movies are most popular? Are they affecting fashion? You bet they are.

The Tudors, The Borgias and The White Queen give us medieval magnificence. Downton Abbey hooked us with Edwardian elegance and Game of Thrones blows us away with chain jewelry, filigree collars and metal couture.

If a piece reminds you of a popular movie or cable series, mention it in your description and ride the trend.

Bohemian or "boho"

This type of adornment is outlandish and colorful. It is multiple bracelets, natural stones, beads, feathers and dangles; it's jewelry that moves when you dance.

It was inspired by the gypsies who inspired the hippies and flower children who *continue to* inspire today's free spirits.

(Boho; had these for years, sold them in 2013)

Goth

Goth jewelry reflects religious and occult themes. Wikipedia tells us it was inspired by Victorian mourning fashions.

(A Goth Couple at Whitby Goth Weekend, photo by Alan Johnson, U.K.; from Wikipedia)

Steampunk

This is a somewhat industrial blend of Edwardian, Victorian, gothic, military and technofantasy. It's goggles and pocket watches, fingerless gloves and cameos.

Helena Bonham Carter wears it well.

Tribal

It's big and bold; the item's roots can be Native American, African, Moroccan, Indian and others.

CHAPTER 10: TAKING PHOTOS

Clear, attractive photos are crucial to selling your jewelry and smalls.

(Sold a few years back; a favorite insect pin with glorious green glass)

Over the years I've come to believe in:

- Flawless close-ups, taken or cropped so that the object takes up the whole of the center
- Indirect natural light
- Invisible or elegant backgrounds (that don't compete for attention)
- Color in cases where the object has none
- Details! Front and back, top and bottom with *special emphasis on markings, clasps and closures*
- At least one photo that demonstrates size

Some people list with eBay's Mobile buying and selling app for iPhone, iPad, Android, BlackBerry and Windows phones.

I downloaded the app, but I only use it for browsing and bidding. I prefer to go old school when listing.

Digital cameras are inexpensive and easy to use. My Panasonic Lumix was about $100. You can be a total geek and read the directions or play with it until you get it right.

Flawless close-ups

I confess, I get a little shaky sometimes. That's bad because *the camera must be perfectly still.*

A **tripod** is (nearly) indispensable for top-down shots. I paid about $20 for a compact aluminum travel model with telescopic legs.

Stacked books are free and they work *extremely* well for taking close photos from lower levels. I like that it's easy to leave one hand free to position or hold the object.

Simply layer books to the desired height and angle the camera. All is secure.

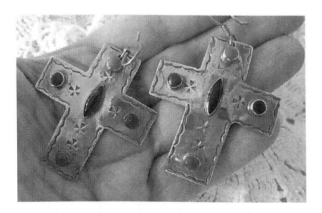

(Sold 2012; Taxco silver earrings with coral & turquoise)

Holding jewelry in the palm of your hand gives it color, warmth and a sense of proportion.

I rest the top of my hand on the table to prevent movement. While you're at it, capture the back for hallmarks, details and patina.

(Clearly marked; the back of Taxco earrings)

You can also put your camera *on* the table to capture detail.

(Sold 2013; vintage scarab ring in silver)

People will see the room beyond, so *prop up the back edge* of the paper or fabric surface to create a distraction-free photo.

Playing with the light

I dangle translucent objects like these antique crystal earrings from my fingers, hang them from props or set them at angles that attract attention.

(Available; a favorite pair of vintage crystal earrings)

Choosing backgrounds

I have black velvet necklace displays for chokers and necklaces, but I (almost) always wind up taking photos of jewelry on white paper or light fabric.

(In storage; white on white, four strands of vintage 50s/60s beads)

Always provide photos of backsides, clasps and closures; they're important for establishing age and quality.

(Omega backs on heavy gold earrings sold in 2012)

Gold and silver can be visually boring. In this photo, the antique surface fabric had a touch of purple and green embroidery at the edges. It was just enough color to attract attention.

I enjoy using exteriors and interiors of old and new jewelry boxes. I staged these earrings *on* an old purple jewelry box.

Dark and jewel tone backgrounds can really make jewelry "pop." The color of the amethysts paired beautifully with the vintage velvet.

It's socially acceptable to use your fingers

Petite earrings may topple without support; gold marks are frequently tucked out of sight in awkward, hard-to-reach areas.

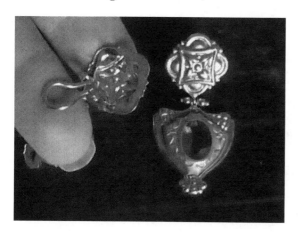

(An old photo; 18k yellow gold earrings with amethyst cabochons)

Taking photos of backs and closures is *especially* important when you don't know what you have!

(Sold to a customer on Central Park West)

Demonstrating size

People *hate* to read descriptions to find sizes and dimensions. You can solve this problem by taking a few photos near a dime, penny, quarter or ruler. In this case I took the photo *on* a dime.

(Using a dime to demonstrate the size of this emerald cut peridot)

Jewelry with interesting elements

If the charms are interesting, take one or more shots *per*.

(This bracelet has one seated Buddha, green glass, snarly dragons & more.)

Do one nice photo with all charms face up and a second with all charms down.

If elements on a necklace or bracelet are fairly complex, keep them in the same exact order when you shoot front and back; that makes it easy for people to know what's what.

Finishing your photos

Take more photos than you need and edit the best with your photo software. In most cases editing involves:

- Cropping each photo to remove unnecessary space
- Tweaking the brightness and contrast to make details easier to see

It's tedious, so take as many breaks as you need. When you're happy with your pictures, you're ready to list.

CHAPTER 11: LISTING YOUR ITEMS

You've done your research, written your description and taken your photos. If you know your price, simply choose the correct category and follow the directions to create your listing.

If you're not sure about price or process, hitch a ride on an existing or completed listing.

Listing from an active or completed item

Let's say you want to list a vintage 14k gold amethyst ring. Search those exact words in All Categories (click Include Description) and – today – eBay delivers 69,970 results as Best Match. That includes new merchandise. You need to drill down.

Choose Vintage & Antique Jewelry from Categories at left and then Ending Soonest; search. You are down to 2,040 listings. From this point search Fine for platinum, gold or silver. (If it's silver or a lesser metal, you would choose Costume. Silver is often listed in either category.)

We'll pretend your amethyst is pear shape. Choose Fine and add "pear shape" to the description and you have 47 results.

Let's see how much they're selling for. Choose Advanced (to the right of the Search bar); click two options – you want to search by Title and Description and Sold Listings.

Fifteen rings have sold. When I'm listing something especially nice, I sort by "Price + Shipping; highest first." *Come to mama ...*

A large, deep purple amethyst sold at Best Offer. $797 is crossed out and the listing notes "Best offer accepted." (Obviously this was a Buy it Now with Best Offer listing.)

A second ring – much less dramatic – sold for $329 as Buy it Now.

If your ring is like any of the rings we see here, you can click the listing and choose "Sell one like this" under the photo at left.

If your photos are ready to go, you can easily create your listing from this one.

Categories

In the case of the ring, the category fits; I can simply edit the title. If not, take time to select the correct category!

Everything we need is under Vintage & Antique Jewelry. Here you will find Costume, Fine, Vintage Ethnic/Regional/Tribal, Vintage Handcrafted, Artisan, New, Vintage Reproductions and miscellaneous other categories.

How important is category?

In November of 2012 I listed an antique citrine and diamond ring in Fine Jewelry. I knew I screwed up when I noticed it wasn't being watched. *It should have been listed in Vintage & Antique Jewelry under Fine – Art Nouveau/Art Deco 1895-1935 – Rings.*

I changed it and the watchers came.

Native American jewelry can be tricky too. I sometimes list under Vintage Ethnic/Regional/Tribal *and* Fine to make sure it gets seen by all the right eyes.

When I list better silver jewelry, I usually list in both Costume and Fine; it's all about anticipating the way people search.

DESCRIBE YOUR ITEM

Title

Use every key search word; you don't need to create a full sentence and you don't need punctuation.

I draw attention by putting key words in caps: "Antique Round BOHEMIAN GARNET CLUSTER RING Size 7 Rose Gold Plated"

If you want to establish yourself as a serious online dealer, avoid irritating space wasters like "LOOK!" or "WOW!!!" They're like putting a bumper sticker on a Mercedes.

Subtitle

If you've done a good job writing the title, you don't need to pay 50 cents for a subtitle.

Condition Description

If it doesn't have defects, ignore. If it does, mention briefly and explain in the description. My charming 1920s pendant had some damage. I wrote: "Is missing a piece of filigree to right of glass." I didn't feel it detracted and the new owner agreed.

(Note missing filigree to right of the glass)

Item Specifics

These are optional and vary per category. Fill in key details and remove anything that's irrelevant. Some specifics allow you to invent your own, as in "May be silver."

ADD PHOTOS

After you've uploaded your photos, take care to choose the best one for your featured photo.

Ask yourself:

- What is this item's most pleasing quality?
- Which photo best represents that quality?

Example: While browsing I saw a photo of an amethyst ring – but it was a top view. All I could see was the main stone. There was no hint of setting, so I assumed it was ordinary.

I happened to click and was shocked to find the base was surrounded by garnets, amethysts and rubies. Despite the low starting price ($36.99) the ring *did not sell.*

If that seller had used one of the better side shots for the featured photo, it would have captured more attention and sold at a very good price.

I remembered that seller's error when I listed this butterscotch agate ring.

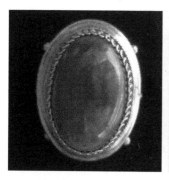 

(The butterscotch agate is marvelous, but the medieval, "Game of Thrones" type side detail makes the ring.)

Add a Description

Use the description you created. (Do not copy words or photos! eBay clearly states that violations of copyright laws can result in listing cancellation, account suspension, loss of PowerSeller status and more.)

I change the font to Georgia and the size to 12 (to ensure it's easy to read.)

If the item has a story, tell it. (Review hints in Chapter 9, *Telling Stories that Sell.*)

I end each description with four key points:

1. Free Domestic Shipping: I pay for shipping and take pains to ship in materials that will protect your purchase.
2. International Shipping: By calculation. Contact me for details.
3. My jewelry comes to you from a non-smoking, dog-loving home.
4. Please see my other unique pieces.

If you decide to charge for shipping, I suggest you add that you will *combine shipping* for multiple purchases.

Listing Designer

I find most designs desperate, distracting or both.

Visitor Counter

The 90s called; they want this feature back.

Choose a format and price

Here you decide between Auction and Buy it Now.

Auctions have an established shelf life of as many days as you choose, usually 7 to 10. If there isn't a seller special, you may pay a listing fee as well as the standard sale fee.

At present there's a special – free listings for 7 day auctions and you only pay if it sells. The Buy it Now format (with or without Best Offer) is 50 cents per month regardless of asking price.

Review the details and determine the "final value fees" for sold items to determine which format you prefer. (I spend more time explaining Buy it Now with Best Offer and standard auctions later in this chapter.)

Select how you'll be paid

I always choose PayPal; it's fast and reliable and I've never had a problem. There is a fee involved, so factor it into your prices. If all this nickel and diming is a little irritating, remember you'd be paying fees for credit card purchases if you had a brick and mortar store.

Add shipping details

I pay U.S. shipping, so my listings look like this:

Flat: same cost to all buyers
USPS First Class Package (2 to 5 business days)
Cost: $0.00
"Free Shipping" is checked
Handling time is 1 business day

If I'm paid by noon, I try to ship same day.

I met a dealer who couldn't believe I ship for free; then he confessed he had problems with his feedback. He said "someone got grumpy about my fees." A customer bought two small items and he charged shipping for both. I would have been grumpy too. *Honorable sellers combine shipping.*

International shipping

Calculated: Cost varies by buyer location. (Choose the countries you are willing to do business with.) I don't charge handling costs for international shipping.

Package details

If you've agreed to international sales, don't be surprised when you receive notice that one of your items sold and you need to send it overseas.

The weight in this section absolutely must be accurate.

Foreign buyers count on the weight you supply when they choose preferred shipping methods. If you underestimate total boxed weight, the additional shipping costs are on you.

When a package is going to be traveling thousands of miles, it needs to be in a sturdy box. Always weigh the item with box and packing materials and *provide the exact weight.*

Don't overestimate weight to make a few extra dollars. If you feel you deserve extra money for more secure packaging, charge handling costs.

Buyer requirements

My requirements block buyers who have received 2 unpaid items strikes within one month; or have a feedback score equal to or lower than -1.

Return policy

I don't normally accept returns because I want to deter impulse buyers. Also, I'm afraid unscrupulous types will swap out stones.

I don't explain my "no refund" policy because eBay tells buyers they're covered anyway.

Current automated wording states "No returns or exchanges, but item is covered by eBay Buyer Protection" (with a link to a full explanation).

I *do* accept returns if I'm concerned about the condition of a piece.

Additional checkout instructions

I usually leave that blank.

Make your listing stand out

No thanks eBay; 50 cents here and there really adds up.

Maximize your listing's visibility

I sometimes add other countries when I'm selling items of international interest. (International buyers find me whether I maximize or not.)

How your listing will appear in search results

This is an important opportunity to confirm you wrote your best heading and featured your best photo.

Review your fees

While we're listing we tend to be optimistic. We may buy additional features, expecting they'll help the item sell quickly. When it doesn't, we may let the listing run and forget about it. We remember when we receive our monthly bill.

Review and remove features you don't *need*.

Preview your listing

I always check for errors. In most cases I should have chosen a better main photo; sometimes I forget to add a ring size in the heading. If there's an error revise; if it's ok, submit. You can still tweak while the item is live.

Congratulations on listing your first item!

Care to list another? If it's like this one, you can simply choose "Sell similar item." The system has saved your preferences.

When your item sells

Don't ship until you've received payment. If I don't receive my money within 24 hours I send an invoice.

Go to your Sold area in My eBay; it's automated.

I include a nice note that thanks them for their purchase and reminds them to look at my other items. This is especially significant when the purchase is going overseas. International buyers pay plenty for shipping; they might as well buy another item while they're at it.

(Language is no problem thanks to eBay's automated translation service.)

Slow pay

If I don't hear back immediately, I assume best intentions. I had unpaid wins when my gall bladder quit in '02; it was four days before I could get back to my emails. People were patient with me, I'm patient with them.

Example: In November of 2012 a buyer won the bid on my antique gold-filled bracelet. She was the *only* bidder and her feedback was perfect.

I sent an invoice and heard nothing.

I know there are a lot of retirees in Phoenix, so I imagined illness or memory issues. I waited another week and wrote asking if she wanted to cancel the bid; still nothing.

Payment arrived a few weeks later. *No big deal.*

No pay

I simply write and ask if they had a change of heart. If they did, I relist. I don't give bad feedback; these are hard times.

When the money hits your account

You will receive notice of payment and eBay will tell you it's ok to ship. *(See Chapter 12: Shipping Sold Items)*

If I'm confident the buyer will be satisfied with the purchase, I transfer funds from PayPal to my checking account; this takes about three days. If it was an expensive item, I wait until the buyer leaves positive feedback.

Feedback

You want to have the last word in every sale. That is – don't leave feedback until you're sure the package arrived and the buyer is happy.

If it didn't and they aren't, they're more likely to work it out peaceably if you retain the upper hand.

Returns

I've only had three. Two were clothing (never again) and one was a vintage ring. There was absolutely nothing wrong with it, the woman was looking for a fight. I didn't take the bait.

I graciously refunded the money and easily sold the ring to a better buyer.

MORE ON BUY IT NOW

If I'm selling something valuable, I choose Buy it Now with Best Offer. People with money want what they want *when they want it*. They don't want to wait and bid with the rabble.

Establishing guidelines

Duration

Your Buy it Now items can run for a specific length of time; or you can choose to let them continue until they sell. That's fine if it's free, but if you're getting charged it can be a problem.

Honestly, *how many times do you want to pay for that item?* The longer it takes, the less you make.

Miminums

Some offers are downright rude; the good news is you don't have to deal with them. You may specify which offers you will accept, which you will consider and which you don't want to see.

For instance, I currently have a historic medal listed on Buy it Now with Best Offer at $45.00. I have it set up so the system will automatically accept any amount over $35.00, but it will ignore anything less than $25.

I can play with that ten dollar gray area, using the counteroffer feature to nudge offers up towards my desired amount.

Before item's end

Before each of my Buy it Now items ends, I check to see if it's being watched. Some watchers will terminate; that's not a big deal. But if you continue to lose watchers, you might want to adjust your listing.

True Story: The Gold Earrings

I listed gold earrings for $500.00; I dropped the price a few times and the value to profit ratio was tight. I specified I would automatically accept any offer over $460 but I didn't want to be bothered with offers under $400.

If an offer within that range arrived, it would be an opportunity to accept, counter-offer or decline. Be careful with negotiations, they can scare the prospect away. On the flip side, don't be a doormat.

After Valentine's Day I received an offer of $450. The woman's note said "If you won't include free shipping at this price, just decline."

(Ouch!)

(These gold earrings were difficult to sell.)

I came very close to accepting, but I decided to check gold prices for that day; the actual value was $540! Add shipping and insurance and her offer would have shorted me $100! But mostly, SHE WAS A SNOT.

I declined and I felt good about it. I left my Buy it Now at $500, but I removed the Best Offer component. The earrings sold within a reasonable period of time to a grateful buyer.

True Story: The Emerald Earrings

In November of 2012 I listed emerald and diamond earrings. You've heard of impulse buys? This was an impulse sale.

Mid-month I heard my third husband was getting remarried. Forget that he drank too much. Forget that 12 years had passed and eight were with another guy. (Me, not him.)

A battle between nostalgia and common sense ensued. *Nostalgia was winning.*

We had only been together three months when he took me on a Caribbean cruise. We viewed every departure from the ship's hot tub. Word in the bubbling waters had it that St. Thomas was THE place to buy emeralds.

I remember thinking that had nothing to do with us. We were just getting to know each other.

When we disembarked, he began to lead me through jewelry stores; *who doesn't dream of a man like this.* One was owned by a soft-spoken Indian gentleman whose kind words stole our hearts. Art bought me a 3 ct. pear cut emerald ring with diamond baguettes.

He was an über generous guy, so I wasn't sure the purchase was socially significant.

As we continued to wander St. Thomas, he turned, kissed me and said "that *is* an engagement ring." I reciprocated by buying him a diamond wedding band; he was so rattled he tripped leaving that store.

I had the distinct impression he was more accustomed to giving than receiving.

We spent our last 90 minutes on St. Thomas at a seaside café, savoring the powerful emotions of an epic day. He slipped away briefly to make a call.

Fifteen minutes later "our" jeweler arrived with a long velvet box filled with emerald and diamond earrings. I was invited to choose a pair that would match my engagement ring.

(Parting with these was painful.)

Sadly, that was then and this was now. I was *nouveau broke*. I never wore the earrings and bills were due.

Did I love my palm trees and beaches? Yes! Did I want to go back to Michigan winters? No! I gently unwrapped them, went to the lanai and took photos on white satin.

How much should I expect to get?

The old appraised value was $2,675.00, but I would be grateful for $2,000. 18k gold had gone way up, diamonds were up – emeralds were about even. What the hell, I would list at the appraised price and negotiate from there.

You know how I drone on about telling stories? I should have waited for a better day to tell this one. It came out pretty pissy. My inner demons convinced my better self that the wording would appeal to the scorned woman demographic.

The following morning I met my friend Connie at Starbucks.

She had just flown in from Toronto and we had two years' worth of catching up to do. I confessed I had gone all sideways over Art's (most recent) remarriage, had listed my magnificent earrings and written an ornery description.

She laughed.

I said I was going to hurry home and edit the description; she said "No, it will probably help you sell!"

I came home to an offer of $1,900! Now note what an asshat I can be. Blinded by greed, I ignored the fact that it was only $100 less than the amount I hoped for; I nearly insisted we meet in the middle.

Fortunately logic won out. It was the end of November and December could be a good month for luxury sales; but I went to My eBay and found *only two people* were watching the earrings.

I sent a counter offer of $2,100, sweetly explaining I would have to pay eBay fees and insured shipping.

Moments later I noticed there had been other offers *under my specified limit*; probably from this person! Maybe $2,000 was all she had to spend and I had ruined my chance for a sale!

The next three hours dragged like three weeks; then I received notice of payment.

The buyer was not the scorned woman I imagined; he was retired military and money *was* an issue. He explained he had bought his wife similar earrings (and a matching ring) many years ago, but they lost them on vacation.

He couldn't wait to surprise her Christmas morning.

I was lucky with those earrings. They sold despite my inappropriate description and the offer was very close to what I wanted; but sometimes we're not so fortunate.

True Story: The Mermaid Lamp

My parents live near Lake Superior. The last time I was there I snooped around their cavernous basement while my jeans clunked around in the dryer.

(The parental units, Bev & John)

It's a dark, moldy, *magical* place where purchases await cleaning or repair before graduating to the glistening glass shelves of their antique shop.

Porcelain fins caught my eye. A mermaid – what a strange thing to find in the U.P.! It was a Capodimonte-style figural lamp with a young fisherman pulling a little blonde mermaid up in his net.

The electrical cord had been cut, but I didn't care. The lamp was SO weird and SO Sanibel. I expected my mother might sell it to me at the customary 7% family discount. To my surprise, she *gave* it to me.

I enjoyed the lamp for a while; then I lost interest. In 2013 the mermaid transitioned from potential decor to permanent storage. My closets are small; it was time for her to go.

(The porcelain lamp with mermaid and fisherman)

Research was difficult because there wasn't anything quite like her. I priced her at $350 on Buy it Now with Best Offer; she didn't have any watchers. I dropped her to $250; one or two watchers. I finally dropped her to $200 and received an offer of $150 from a lady in New York. I accepted.

You're thinking I'm the world's worst daughter because my mother GAVE me that lamp. You have to understand that I've walked into her shop to *find personal gifts from me* on *her* shelves!

For Christmas 2012 I struggled to find something she might like; I finally found an opulent piece of souvenir glass (with heavy gold leaf) from the town where she and my stepdad married.

I left the price tag on for her convenience.

Anyway … shipping the lamp was a pain, with those delicate fins and fragile fingers. *(See Chapter 12: Shipping Sold Items)*

I wound up taking the box to FedEx; that cost more than $30.

When all was said and done, I made enough to pay the Comcast bill.

True Story: The Disney Trinket Box

Sometimes we're better off using Buy it Now *without* Best Offer. The best feature of this little box was the sweet blue tile of Thumper, the bunny from Bambi.

(The Disney Trinket Box with Thumper)

Despite proper storage, the tile was yellowing; it's alarming how climate can affect the condition of aging materials.

It had a few watchers initially – but they went away.

I lowered the price from $45 to $35 *without* Best Offer and Thumper sold quickly.

MORE ON EBAY AUCTIONS

Auctions attract bargain hunters and bottom feeders. I put items out to auction when I'm willing to list low and sell low. There's a chance a bidding war will ensue, but I don't count on it.

So why do it? Because it's great bait. Cheap merchandise can attract prospective buyers to your better merchandise.

At one point I had four fairly expensive items in Buy it Now with Best Offer – but very few watchers. I started sending lesser items to auction, wrote "see my other items" in my descriptions and the number of watchers increased quickly.

The better pieces sold, making my sacrifices worthwhile.

Remembering time zones

These days smartphones and devices put bidding capabilities at buyers' fingertips any place and any time; but there are many who are reluctant to embrace the latest technologies.

I schedule items so traditional types have time to bid. I'm in Florida, but most of my buyers are in California and New York. I list my 7 day auctions mid to late afternoon on Saturday or Sunday; that way I'm not too early or late for either coast.

Listing on Saturday or Sunday gives people with jobs an opportunity to spot the merchandise during the work week and the weekend to pay attention to the bid.

Payment usually arrives within 24 hours. That gives me Sunday to print shipping labels and wrap and Monday morning to walk them out to the mailbox.

Buyers are dazzled by my speed, when it's really *so* easy.

Making the most of the holidays

We've talked about listing before the holidays. Be especially careful about timing when you've selected auction format. The listing must allow the buyer time to pay for, receive, wrap and give the gift.

(I purchased these red padded bracelet boxes on eBay.)

I recommend stating you will be sending the item in a gift box. It's one less thing for them to buy during the holiday rush – *and one more reason to buy from you.*

Sales heat up in the winter

But they can be dismal on Easter, Fourth of July, Memorial Day and Labor Day; people tend to go on vacation during warm weather.

MINDING YOUR LISTINGS

It becomes part of your daily rhythms. When I'm in active selling mode, I wake up and – still in bed – reach for my tablet to check on sales, Best Offers and questions.

Sales

People who pay full price (without Best Offer negotiation) make my day. I return the favor by shipping immediately.

If I'm especially happy I pay a little more for Priority Flat Rate; it faster and includes $50 in insurance for "mailpieces with barcodes." (We automatically provide barcodes when we print our labels.)

Best offers

Prospect desire can fade quickly, so accept or negotiate at once.

Remember the green enamel earrings? When my buyer received them, she wrote to say she was SO glad I accepted because she had just put an offer in on another pair. She wrote "I like these better!"

If I hadn't been on top of my emails, I would have lost that sale.

Questions

People usually write within an hour of the item's end to ask about international shipping. Go to usps.com. Choose "Calculate a Price," then – under "Select a Destination" – choose the country and supply details.

Thanks to the United States Postal Service, international shipping as easy as local shipping.

I feel most confident recommending Priority Mail International Small Flat Rate Box. It gets the item to the buyer within 6 to 10 business days and supplies are FREE.

You can have Priority Mail boxes (in a variety of sizes) delivered to your home through usps.com.

When your buyer chooses a less expensive shipping method, you supply the box; make sure it's sturdy!

My last international sale went to Russia; I was a little bit freaked that she chose cheaper shipping. It took weeks to get there, but she was kind enough to write and thank me, saying her bracelet arrived safely.

Example: **Earrings to Israel**

The agates were stunning, but I wasn't sure the earrings would sell because they had screwbacks. About an hour before the auction's end, a woman wrote asking how much it would cost to ship to Israel.

(Agate earrings with screwbacks)

I answered quickly; she won the bid and paid immediately – including $16.95 for shipping.

That night I chose a gift box for the earrings, attached a thank-you note, wrapped it in tissue, printed the shipping label and taped it to a Priority Flat Rate box.

I went to usps.com to arrange for pickup.

In the morning I walked the package out to the mailbox and watched the postal worker scan it before she drove away.

Example: **Mexican silver to the Netherlands**

An hour before the auction was scheduled to end, I received an email asking how much it would cost to ship my Taxco shell pendant to the Netherlands.

(Taxco silver shell pendant)

I gave her shipping choices, responding: "Hi Karen: Shipping to the Netherlands via Priority Mail® International Small Flat Rate Box is $16.95 and will take approximately 6 to 10 days. First Class is $8.46, but the United States Postal Service doesn't say when the package would arrive.

If you win the bid, let me know which you prefer. I combine shipping if you're interested in my other items. Sincerely, Micki"

I gave Karen what I considered to be the best option *as well as* a cheaper alternative. Her English was excellent. If the individual is struggling to communicate, keep your choice of words as basic as possible.

(As previously stated, eBay's translation option works *surprisingly* well!)

108

When items don't sell

If an item doesn't sell, you can simply relist.

If nobody is *watching* the item, consider:

- Replacing photos or adding new
- Putting it out to auction at the lowest price you will accept
- Lowering the price on Buy it Now with Best Offer option
- Lowering the price on Buy it Now *without* the Best Offer option
- Ending the listing for the time being

If you decide to end a listing, keep a copy of the description so it will be easy to relist.

CHAPTER 12: SHIPPING SOLD ITEMS

Make sure the customer has paid before you ship; eBay will tell you when the funds have landed in your account.

If the funds arrive early I try to ship same day; if not, I get the package ready that night for shipment the following morning.

I hate to go to the post office, so I have a scale for weighing packages and a printer for creating labels.

Recommended shipping supplies include:

- Small and medium boxes, usually recycled; or new 4x4x4
- Paper grocery bags for covering recycled boxes that have writing, labels and old barcodes; cut, cover and securely tape
- Priority Mail Small Flat Rate boxes; they work for U.S. and international shipping and are free from your local post office or usps.com
- Adhesive tape and clear packaging tape; buy the good stuff, the cheap brands are more trouble than they're worth
- Padded envelopes (big enough for gift boxes)
- Gift boxes or …
- Clean cardboard for cutting, shaping and taping custom-sized protective boxes for shipping jewelry in padded envelopes
- Bubble wrap or tissue; you don't want your goods flopping around en route and you don't want your customer opening a box that rattles

As you can see, much of what we need is free.

Take time to harvest the best of the debris from showers, weddings and holidays; that includes festive ribbons, colorful tissue, nice boxes and premium packaging materials.

Consider the safety of each item before you ship.

For instance, when I have earrings with posts that might scratch each other during shipping, I wrap each separately.

Why buy gift boxes?

Mainly because they protect fragile jewelry when you ship in envelopes! I've won bids on vintage jewelry that arrived crushed in flat envelopes. In one case a seller sent several antique crystal necklaces – strung on wire – in a padded envelope; they arrived hopelessly mangled.

But there are other reasons. Fresh new gift boxes:

- Can be a great way to stage your merchandise in photos.
- Feed anticipation as the buyer knows exactly what to expect.
- Offer convenience and savings when the customer is buying as a gift.
- Honor and delight your customer on delivery.
- Make the merchandise seem *more special*.
- Make you seem *more professional*.

I have several types and sizes; I prefer my satin padded bracelet boxes for brooches, necklaces and more. You can find a nice selection on eBay under "Retail and Services" – "Jewelry Packaging & Display."

Finishing touches

For an extra measure of professionalism, you might also consider:

- Gift boxes or silk string pouches
- Colorful wrapping tissue
- Attractive note paper

I try to coordinate packing materials, from magenta tissue to matching thank-you notes.

(Silk pouch with gift box & thank-you note)

I fuss over presentation because I am *so* grateful the buyer chose *my* merchandise out of everything available on eBay.

Printing shipping labels

eBay has this down to a science. Simply go to the sold item and choose "Print Label." The system will guide you through choice of shipping; just purchase postage and print.

Other advantages to eBay's automated labels:

- In some cases postage costs less online.
- It's easy to add insurance.
- The system automatically notifies the buyer that the package is on its way.
- We save money on gas.
- There's no standing in line at the post office.

I always apply clear tape over the address portion of each label to prevent damage from rain, snow, etc. *Do not tape over bar codes.*

Mailing expensive jewelry

I prefer Small Flat Rate Priority Mail with insurance.

I line the shipping box with wrapping tissue, fold it over the gift box, place the thank-you note on top and press the edges to make sure they seal properly.

Mailing less expensive merchandise

I put the item in a gift box, place a thank-you note on top, wrap lightly with thin bubble wrap (so the edges won't bust through the envelope) and place in a padded envelope.

Print the label and tape it to the envelope *before* you insert the box; it's easier to tape to a flat surface and looks more professional.

I ship these items First Class Package; jewelry in a gift box usually weighs around 2 to 3 ounces.

IMPORTANT!

The post office considers an envelope *with bulk* a package, so use that rate when calculating shipping.

If you mail by hand – that is, don't print the label on eBay – take a moment to go back online and mark the item "shipped;" the system will notify your buyer that the package is on its way.

Shipping unusual shapes and larger items

When in doubt, see how other sellers are shipping that type of merchandise.

When backed into a corner, I use the shipping stores.

You can walk in with your box ready to go and ask which shipping method is best; or you can walk in with the item, in which case you will be charged for packaging materials and box.

True Story: Shipping the Mermaid Lamp

Selling it was only *half* of the problem.

I wrapped the lamp *mummy style* in recycled bubble wrap and made sure it was protected from every angle.

The only box I had was from nuts.com; it was covered with goofy slogans and the lamp just barely fit. I wrapped it in brown paper Publix grocery bags (turned inside out and neatly trimmed).

It was going to New York City; I imagined a smart, sophisticated buyer weeping with laughter.

I used generous quantities of tape and wrote the address and "FRAGILE" in magic marker – (like the leg lamp in The Christmas Story); but I was still nervous about the safety of the contents.

Finally I gave up and went to the shipping store. An associate suggested we put my box in a larger box with Styrofoam peanuts.

I paid $7 for additional packing materials, $3.00 for insurance and $21.38 for shipping. That's right, $31.38; *argh*. But I knew the lamp would arrive intact.

I went home and added the tracking information to the transaction so the buyer would know it was on its way.

She left great feedback.

Shipping pictures and paintings

Years ago I sold antique pictures and paintings on eBay; framed pictures with glass were especially tricky. I wrapped them in bubble wrap and double boxed, bunching newspapers at the outside edges of the interior box.

They always arrived safely.

You can find calculated rates per weight online at the shipper's website.

Save money by recycling

Consider saving these for future use:

- Boxes of all shapes and sizes; don't forget the box within a box approach to shipping fragile merchandise
- Paper grocery bags; wrap and tape around busy boxes
- Tissue from wedding and showers; I love the thought of customers opening a boring box to a burst of color
- Shipping peanuts
- Cardboard – bend, cut and tape to create new boxes; or use bent pieces to help protect fragile items

Recycling – it's better for the planet *and* your bank account.

CHAPTER 13: LEARN MORE ON EBAY

If you want to get serious about selling jewelry, historical or other collectibles online, it *pays* to become an expert.

Begin your adventure with eBay searches; you never know what might turn up.

When I search live items, I always include Title and Description; this can currently be found in Advanced Search, to the right of the Search bar. Then I choose Ending Soonest instead of Best Match; it's under Sort beneath the Search bar.

Choose the best Category to drill down.

When you find an item you like, click Add to Watch, upper right under the title. That saves the item to My eBay.

To review, My eBay is your base of operations. It maintains information on all of your activity – from what you're watching to how many people are watching YOUR items.

Save your best search terms

Every now and then we discover great new search terms. Let's say you found an antique citrine ring by searching "yellow glass" in Vintage & Antique Jewelry; how addictive is that!

Save the search term by choosing Advanced (next to the Search bar) and Save This Search to My eBay. eBay will deliver your saved search results to your inbox every morning.

You'll find more in-depth information on search methods in Finding Inventory in Chapter 14.

LEARN MORE ONLINE

These are some of my favorite sources.

Antique Jewelry University

As stated earlier, it's one of the most comprehensive online reference sites I've found. See www.antiquejewelryuniversity.com

Collectors Weekly

Collectors Weekly – www.collectorsweekly.com – is another outstanding free resource. See the "Jewelry & Watches" category to find the "Antique Fine Jewelry" and "Costume Jewelry" sections.

"Show & Tell" allows people to upload pictures of mystery items, hoping to find answers; and top eBay auctions are featured.

When you relate to a specific topic, you can sign up for that section's newsletter. (Choose "Get weekly email.")

Collector Books online

Collector Books on collectibles (jewelry, dishes, glassware and more) have been a favorite reference for many years; unfortunately, they suspended publication in August of 2012.

Find them as eBooks at www.collectorbooks.com

I prefer their hard cover books. If you're lucky enough to find them, I encourage you to buy the ones that interest you, flip through occasionally and *fill your brain* with pictures and facts. They'll help you recognize unmarked pieces and better styles in the field and online.

Your subconscious will tell you when it's ok to spend a little more.

LEARN MORE ON DEMAND

PBS is the Mother Lode.

Watch **Antiques Roadshow** every chance you get. I appreciate that they've edited some of the older shows to demonstrate how values have increased or decreased.

If you're a history and fine antique freak, **Antiques Roadshow U.K.** may well blow your mind. The locations and finds are phenomenal.

I was never a big fan of **Market Warriors**; the concept of buying at established shows and flea markets to sell at established auctions is ludicrous. High profile antique shows and flea markets often have prices as high as antique shops and auctions are a total crap shoot. When the warriors' finds (regularly) crashed at auction, I felt their pain.

But the show is still available on demand; the competition and camaraderie give it entertainment value.

Visit www.pbs.org – choose Programs.

History.com is excellent too.

Pawn Stars is entertaining and informative. Three generations of the Harrison family, owners of the Gold & Silver Pawn Shop near Las Vegas, work to assess, buy and sell some really unusual stuff; some of it historical.

American Pickers makes me miss "picking" for my shop. Wikipedia explains: "Wolfe and Fritz explore people's homes, barns, sheds, and other outbuildings, and other places where they have stored antiques and collectibles. They call upon casual collectors, hoarders and occasionally people who have inherited overwhelming collections of apparent junk."

Visit www.history.com – choose Shows.

CHAPTER 14: BUYING ONLINE TO SELL ONLINE

This is my joy. This is me at the casino hanging at the quarter slots.

I tend to spend about $25 per item. If I buy properly, I can relist for double or triple; most working people can afford jewelry between $50 and $75.

Many sellers throw goods up with tacky titles, silly asterisks and inappropriate use of caps. They can't spell, take inferior photos and won't spend two seconds on research.

Some don't know garnets from rhinestones or amethysts from purple glass.

God help me, I do love them.

(Aqua glass bracelet; purchased online to sell online)

When you see an item you like, click "Add to Watch List."

FINDING INVENTORY

These are my three favorite ways to find merchandise for resale:

1: New Searches

Begin by looking under Vintage & Jewelry (Costume) categories. Always search Title and Description, Ending Soonest and scroll; it's exciting to see what's selling for big money, what's selling dirt cheap and what's being utterly ignored.

"Watch" items you like and check on watched items regularly. There is nothing more frustrating than forgetting to bid and going back to My eBay to find the item sold for the starting price.

2: Saved Searches

If you have saved searches, eBay works while you sleep, scouring thousands of listings to deliver "New items that match" to your email inbox.

These emails may also feature "Popular items on eBay." We're programmed to ignore ads; don't do that here. eBay uses your search preferences to recommend similar items.

3: My Feed

This service – which appears on your eBay homepage after sign-in – has bigger photos, so it's the more visual way to browse. *I consider it the most powerful tool in my eBay arsenal.* I've found many items I would have missed otherwise.

There's an urgency to it. I have purchased inadequately or improperly described items *within minutes* of their being listed. I strike as others contemplate.

These search methods do *more* than help us find unusual new pieces.

They:

- Improve our visual assessment skills
- Add to our overall knowledge of estate jewelry
- Offer details we can use to improve the descriptions of our own merchandise
- Provide real-world pricing information

You may already have a drawer like mine – full of questionable or completely unknown pieces. The answers will come as you continue to employ these three methods.

In time you'll start having full blown "Omigod" moments.

True Story: The Elusive Catholic Martyr

My most recent My Feed find was simply listed "chunky vintage bracelet;" it was, in fact, much more.

Remember what I said about making sure you have a good photo of every charm? This bracelet was arranged so that someone would have had to be able to recognize Joan of Arc on sight from any angle.

She was *upside down and squeezed into the corner of the frame.*

The epic Catholic martyr was SO easy to miss and she was absolutely the most important charm on the bracelet. Other elements included mounted knights, art glass and faux pearls.

One red flag – the listing said the bracelet was old and had wear. Heck, it looked good to me.

The seller's profile showed she deals in a variety of items, mostly clothing and books. She does *not* specialize in estate jewelry.

The seller had the bracelet at $25.00 in Buy it Now with Best Offer. I offered $20 and immediately felt guilty.

What a bloodsucker, antique dealer thing to do; find a screaming deal and negotiate.

A few hours later she counter-offered $23.50. I responded by paying full price; my karmic burden eased a bit.

The bracelet arrived in clumsily folded white paper with crooked staples at each edge. She scribbled "Thank You" on top; like she could barely be bothered.

But there were several pleasant surprises. The bracelet's chain doesn't have condition issues; the antique look of the metal is part of the design and I happen to love it. The seller stated that the bracelet was Germany, but she didn't bother to look at the back of the charms. The Joan of Arc pendant is by ART – a popular designer.

A quick search revealed that the pendant alone – with all rhinestones and faux pearls present – is valued at about $65.00! Unfortunately that's not the case with *this* charm/pendant. Now I know why Joan was angled and almost out of frame! Two faux seed pearls and one rhinestone are missing. Bad seller! *Deceptive* seller!

She thought she got me, but she didn't know what she had and the price was right. I left Joan as-is, described fully and listed at a fair price. I think she'll sell just fine.

(Joan of Arc, missing seed pearls and a rhinestone)

Time well spent

I was able to spot Joan of Arc *upside down in a corner* because I spend so much time using eBay's powerful automated search tools. Going through saved search emails and the latest listings on My Feed takes nearly two hours every morning, but it's worth every minute.

I also appreciate these searches because they help me know if my prices are in line. They need to be because ...

Competition is fierce

I pass on extreme deals on average items; I'd rather sell unusual pieces that stop me in my tracks.

One of my saved searches is for "Agate." I found a pendant that had nine glorious bezel-set agates in an Etruscan type setting. The description read: "Unusual folk art look pendant necklace w round bezel set genuine stones."

(Tribal style agate pendant stamped "India")

I won it for the base listing price – $6.99; shipping was free.

Shortly after paying, I searched "carnelian agate pendant" to see if there was anything similar and found an *identical* pendant. It was listed as "EXTREME RARE Vintage India/Chinese Pendant of Carnelian Agate Cabochons."

The seller had premium merchandise, the photos were exceptional and the Buy it Now price (without Best Offer to cushion the blow) was $162.50. I priced mine a little less *with* Best Offer.

As prices rise on watched items

If they're modest, I continue to watch. If they're rising out of reach, I end the Watch; or I may hang out to see what the item sells for. Knowledge of current values helps us buy more wisely.

After the auction, final prices can be found in your My eBay Watch List under Ended items.

Browse worldwide

Don't restrict your searches to the United States; shipping isn't all that much. An all-time favorite purchase was a lot of antique religious charms from a dealer in Belgium.

(Pardon the old photo; this bracelet began as a lot of loose medals from Belgium.)

I know I bought right when I have trouble parting with my purchase. When the medals arrived, I went through, set unattractive/corroded pieces aside, organized the ones I liked and attached them to a premium vintage silver bracelet.

I included the largest medal as a pendant and made a nice profit. (I could have attached a suitable chain and sold it separately.)

What to look for

We tend to buy and sell what we love. I'm always looking for jewelry with:

- Dragons
- Missing stones; *I know a jeweler who can fix that*
- Spiritual or historical significance
- Fancy fobs with cabochons
- Art glass, agate, or stone on silver
- Purple glass that is amethyst or amethyst glass
- Deep red glass that is bohemian garnet
- Faux turquoise or turquoise glass that is Peking glass

I also like to find charm bracelets with:

- Gaps and clumping; all I need to do is rearrange
- Charms that are worth more than the bracelet; I'll sell those separately
- Bracelets that are better than their charms; I remove the charms and sell the bracelet by itself – or add more desirable charms

I've seen nice rings where the seller could only guess at the size. People walk away or bid less because they assume they'll have to pay a jeweler to resize.

Those listings are good opportunities because I'm *not* buying for myself and *I have a ring sizer*! I'll take better photos, list the size and sell to whoever it fits!

Take advantage of inadequate descriptions.

I saw a Lisner brooch with a beautiful helmeted figure. Male or female, history or myth? I didn't know; but I do have smart friends.

I put the link on Facebook, asked for assistance and they hunted it down for sport.

(This image looked familiar, but I was clueless.)

He is Hermes, a mythical being with significant powers; a good luck piece. I bid, won and should have no problem selling him!

Look for anything unusual or attractive that's priced too cheap.

Find out why; the seller may be hoping for a bidding war while prospects steer clear of a deal that seems too good to be true. (I've landed a few of those. It doesn't happen often, but it does happen.)

The item may not have bids because of bad timing.

In the summer months the people who buy jewelry tend to be outside with their families – away from their computers and not quite as dependent on their smartphones.

Pay attention to bad photos.

A busy bracelet on a leopard print is your "what the heck is that?!" moment; you have an edge because most people won't bother to take a closer look. Same goes for *anything* with awful pictures!

Deal breakers

These are personal prejudices. I realize some sellers do just fine selling this sort of thing, but I avoid:

- Unmarked gold; it can be hard to sell without an appraisal.
- Plastics and Lucite; I know some types are very popular. I don't like the way they look or feel – they have always seemed cheap.
- Anything with a lot of rhinestones; they tend to discolor with age and when they fall out, it can be hard to find an exact match.
- Expandable and stretch type jewelry; I assume it won't hold up.
- Lack of wear or patina suggests it could be a reproduction.

Wear that's consistent with age is ok.

Reviewing Listings

Beware of …

Inflated shipping rates

If the price seems too good to be true, check the shipping cost; it may be more than the item. Predatory sellers continue to use shipping as a profit center.

Exaggeration and misrepresentation

Read every word. The vintage watch was three days from end of auction. The title advertised "Vintage 14k White Gold Ladies Rolex 1960s Dress Watch."

The description declared "EXCELLENT CONDITION*** ELEGANT PERFECTION***ROLEX"

God I hate caps and asterisks; but I digress.

The photos were especially handsome; to all outward appearances this was a gold Rolex watch. It was 3 days from conclusion with 36 bids at only $260! That figure would skyrocket at the end.

Seemed like a bargain – except for one thing. I read the whole description and discovered:

"Total weight: 9.2 grams"
"Bracelet material: Speidel flex strap"

Well hold on a darned minute. This was not a Rolex watch! It was a Rolex HEAD. That 9.2 grams was mostly Speidel watch band – inexpensive goldtone metal, not gold.

A new Speidel flex strap is about $19.00. A genuine 14k gold Rolex band starts at over $1,000.

This was a fairly new seller, only 101 transactions with 99% feedback. I didn't follow to see what it sold for.

eBay virgins

Many newbies don't know what they're doing. That can be a good thing – or it can be a disaster.

True Story: The Antique Print

I watched an antique print of Sir Thomas Wyatt the Poet go through three auction cycles. The photo was a little blurry, but I knew the image by heart. I was hoping it would still be available when I had extra cash.

The price was excellent – less than $100 – but there were red flags. He was charging too much money to ship what was essentially a piece of paper WITHOUT frame and glass.

When I had extra cash I decided to risk it. Within a week an enormous box arrived by UPS. This guy spent about $20 on bubble wrap; it *reeked* of cigarette smoke.

What I assumed was a poor photo was a moldy old print on spongy, substandard materials.

The bubble wrap was the best part of that purchase. I aired it out on the lanai for several days, sprayed it with Febreze and it came in handy when I shipped the mermaid lamp.

I don't expect I'll ever frame the print. I left good feedback, but pitched a bitch one on one.

If I had checked his other items I would have realized he didn't know a thing about antique prints.

Iffy feedback

I usually buy from sellers with 99% positive feedback or better.

If the item is irresistible, I may take chances on a seller with spotty feedback.

True Story: The Buddha Bracelet

Buddha bracelets with faux jade sell well. I was watching one with a starting price of 99 cents. This was a $70 bracelet; surely it wouldn't go for a dollar!

I wanted to bid, but I didn't like the seller's feedback. I took a closer look. An early comment revealed that someone won a very low bid and the seller did not follow through. A battle ensued; but that was three years ago; she was new then. Most everything since had been positive.

They say Americans love a comeback. I felt bad about her rocky start, admired her taste and liked the item enough to bid.

I was poised to strike – in the last 10 seconds I submitted a bid of $36.00. Darned if I didn't win the bracelet for 99 cents! I was the only bid; I felt *awful.*

I wrote and told her so, offering to pay an extra $10 for shipping. She declined and said she knew the risks when she listed; but she must have been pleased by my offer because the bracelet arrived in a silk purse wrapped in a bright blue bow – with free earrings to match.

Old jewelry in small sizes

People are bigger than they used to be.

I found a vintage sterling silver, double link charm bracelet at a great price; then I saw it was only 6" long. That's a problem because most women wear 7" or better.

I'm not sure an extender would work with this type of bracelet. *Pass.*

I saw an interesting bookchain necklace with metal leaves; it was only 14" long. *Pass.*

Neck sizes, wrist sizes, ring sizes; why is truly old jewelry so *small?*

According to Laura Blue's 2008 article on Time.com, *Why Are People Taller Today Than Yesterday;* "We have been increasing in height for about 140 years. Prior to that, there were cycles in height, depending on economic circumstances and agricultural productivity and so forth.

We were relatively tall in the Middle Ages, when population densities were relatively low and food supplies were still fairly adequate.

The low point was in the 17th century. ... Only since about the middle of the 19th century has there been a general trend upwards."

(Laura Blue is a senior contributing health writer for TIME.com.)

Embellished items

Yeah, I know; this makes me sound like a hypocrite. I talk about the importance of knowing how to fix and embellish; but any time you add elements to an old piece, the piece is no longer original.

"OOAK" is "one of a kind;" that means an artist or jewelry maker has gone crazy making new jewelry from vintage elements. Many are bracelets made of 50s earrings. Their work is dazzling, but good luck reselling; vintage purists won't touch it.

I've also noticed a flood of bookchain necklaces with beads. No, most *did not* come like that.

Note that I have purchased lovely vintage jewelry that had no color, added colorful beads and sold it online. (Color sells.) This has worked for me when it's a silvertone or goldtone bracelet with many leaves.

If I make changes to a piece, I'm honest about it.

INSPECTING PHOTOS

View *every* photo *every* time.

Sellers may be up front about damage in the description or you may discover problems in their photos.

It was a fancy silver signet ring and I *had* to have it. No bids – *how odd*. The featured photo was outstanding and the seller had nearly 1,000 transactions with 100% positive feedback.

I nearly bid on trust.

There was nothing worrisome in "Item condition." However, the seller wrote "the adjustable section is *not exactly round* anymore."

Are you kidding me? Based on the additional photos, it never *was* an adjustable ring. The back had been cut and the shape was hopelessly mangled; it was in no condition to be worn.

Does the photo match the description?

Sellers don't always take time to know what they're selling; even sellers with thousands of transactions.

I found an item listed as a "Greek coin." It's an ancient coin – or an old copy of an ancient coin – but it's absolutely not Greek.

It has the ancient symbol of the Knights Templar. Properly listed, the seller could have done very well with this coin; instead of nearly "giving" it to me.

Look for condition/repair issues

If I like it and know I can fix it, I buy it! I know how to replace rhinestones, replace vintage clasps and restring necklaces. (This is why I say it's worth your while to take a beading or jewelry making class.)

You might also purchase the item if you have a good, affordable jeweler standing by.

Beware of repros.

Most truly vintage jewelry has a patina! You *need* to see back, clasps and mechanisms! Knowledgeable dealers *know* that. If you only see a photo of the front, ask for a variety of shots.

Reproduction jewelry is everywhere. Beware of terms like "vintage *style*" and "vintage *look*." At least this person listed properly:

"925 SILVER GENUINE GREEN PERIDOT ANTIQUE VINTAGE REPRODUCTION RING SIZE 7"

He or she put "reproduction" in the title and listed in the "New Vintage Reproductions" sub-category. Unfortunately, I have seen repros listed in *every* Vintage & Antique Jewelry sub-category.

eBay doesn't have authenticity cops, so we must be vigilant. I've seen sellers attempt to pass newer Tibetan turquoise and silver jewelry off as vintage southwest or Native American.

When you think about specializing in certain types of jewelry, it's worth your while to get acquainted with similar offerings – old and new – before you start buying.

Extreme close-ups

Objects in photos may be *much smaller* than they appear.

In 1998 I bid on – and won – a topaz brooch; imagine my horror when it arrived, smaller than a dime. I can't sell it and I won't wear it. I only made that mistake once.

Digital cameras take such amazing close-ups it's easy to forget we're getting a gnat's eye view.

When fabric threads look like docking ropes and lint is as big as boulders, we need to look for the actual size in the written description.

I also appreciate sellers who put a coin near the object; it's a visually convenient way to demonstrate proportion.

I do the same in many of my listings.

(Vintage necklace with faux sapphires and pearls)

BEFORE YOU BID

Check the seller's other listings. If their wares are suspicious, you know to back off. If you find they don't specialize in jewelry, you may be in for a bargain.

True Story; The Dragon Ring

I won a bid on an antique ring with a sapphire blue cabochon and dragons.

I wasn't sure what I was getting because the pictures were awful and the seller didn't know the size; but it felt like a good bet because *his other listings were car parts.*

I couldn't wait for my win to arrive. When it did, I tore into the package with my teeth. Rather than put the ring in a box in a padded envelope, he stuffed it in wad upon wad of old padded envelopes.

But it's lovely and the size is petite! Victorian maybe? The stone may even be real. I have research to do.

This gamble was worth the bet.

Interested in more than one item?

See if they combine shipping. If you can't tell from the listing, write and ask. Most sellers are happy to wait a bit longer for payment on multiples.

Save favorite sellers

If you love the seller's taste, opt to Save This Seller so you can see what he or she sells down the line.

WINNING THE BID

If you've read the whole description, checked shipping prices, examined every photo and reviewed the seller's other items, you are ready to go.

I believe in three bidding approaches.

1. Sniping

That is, waiting until the last 5-8 seconds and entering the most money you're willing to spend. I snipe when the item is unique, difficult to identify and likely to get hit hard with hopeful bids those last few seconds. (But be careful. I've waited so long I've shut myself out.)

When you snipe and win, you only pay a small increment above the previous highest bid. If you get outbid, take comfort in knowing you stood your ground. We're in this to make money, not lose it.

2. Marking

It's an early bid – a low-ish bid. It's cheapskate v. cheapskate in a battle of the tightwads.

Let's say the seller has many items out at $9.99 and most of the listings are being ignored. You know you can resell the item for $25 or more because you've learned to see what the general eBay population *does not see.*

Best of all, you like it but you don't LOVE it. Well, you love it if you can get it for $12 with free shipping.

Placing a $12 bid about an hour or two before the listing's end is you marking your territory, you as the rattlesnake in the weeds, shaking your tail – stay away! For all they know, your bid was $75.

The worst that can happen is you can get outbid.

136

3. Making an offer

Remember My Feed earlier in the *Finding Inventory* section of this chapter? It's on your eBay homepage, full of fresh listings with big photos that make it easy to identify cool stuff. Many of those items are in the Buy it Now with Best Offer category.

I usually make an offer that's 15 to 20% lower than the asking price. As a seller, I'm insulted by lesser offers.

When you win

Please pay immediately. Sellers include the chronically ill, veterans, retirees and others who are desperate for this income.

Print or copy the seller's description for your records; you'll need it when you relist. Don't forget to add the total price, item and shipping.

Leave feedback after you receive your item.

If I'm pleased I write "great seller, unique merchandise" or "better than described, highly recommend."

If I have a problem with a purchase, I don't give negative feedback; I write and tell the seller what went wrong.

When you buy from a newbie

Ship happens.

Winning an amazing piece of jewelry from a new seller is nerve-wracking. There's a good chance they'll wrap your purchase in paper towel and ship in a manila envelope.

The potential for damage is worse if they try to save money by shipping as an "envelope" instead of "package." I've been told the post office piles the poundage on plain envelopes, whereas an envelope with contents – *a package* – is treated with care.

I usually send an email right away.

"You appear to be a new seller. Please ship my earrings as a package, not an envelope and put them in a small box instead of wrapping them in tissue.

If you don't have a box, please cut cardboard, bend it into box shape and tape securely so they won't get crushed. Thanks so much."

You might even offer to pay a few extra dollars for careful packaging. Most new sellers appreciate gentle guidance.

If you forgot to bid

Be cool; if nobody wins or buys, the seller usually relists.

With Buy it Now items, eBay will send you an email stating you have another chance to buy.

RELISTING WINS & PURCHASES

A good win is your opportunity to:

- Take more appealing photos
- Do meaningful research
- Write a more thorough description and …
- Make better profit!

The goal is to double or triple your investment.

When I acquire good items for low prices, I usually put them out to auction at a little more than double the starting bid; as in buying for $10, including shipping, and relisting with a starting bid of $25. That pretty much covers eBay fees.

(I expect to double my money on the Joan of Arc bracelet.)

When I get *great items* for *very low* prices, the price can easily be triple or more.

Over time you'll develop an eye for the good stuff. You'll know what certain styles are selling for and feel confident about spending – and listing for – more money.

I sell better merchandise via Buy it Now with Best Offer.

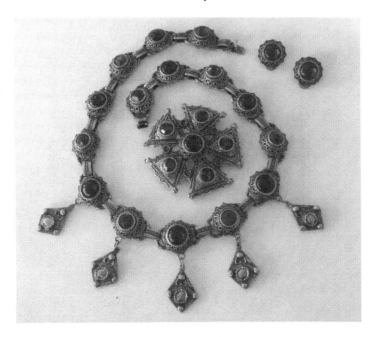

(SOLD: This unsigned purchase was spectacular in person)

When I think it might sell in Europe, I pay a little extra for "International site visibility." You'll find it under "Maximize your listing's visibility" on the listing form.

(It's something you can go back and add later.)

When we don't achieve our goals

We won't always double our investment every time; that's ok. We can usually make up for it on another item. *It balances out.*

CHAPTER 15: BUYING OFFLINE TO SELL ONLINE

That which sucks from the selling perspective can be a winner when you go to buy. I have been ripped off selling at auction, but I've bought well by knowing how to spot good antique jewelry in a tray full of ordinary pieces.

Once in a while, we may even nab a bargain at an established antique shop.

True Story: The Dragon Bracelet

There's an interesting antique shop on the way to Fort Myers Beach. Their prices rarely leave enough room to make money, but I like their selection and their silky gray shop cat.

They keep their jewelry in one of those turntable displays. I was pressing the button when this bracelet came into view.

The glass was perfection and the dragons were magnificent.

The tag said $18; I had $15 in cash. The owner accepted my offer. It quickly sold for over $100.

I'm still kicking myself for that one. I should have waited until I knew what it was. (To be honest, I still haven't found anything like it.) But it was summer; sales were slow and I had bills to pay. I love that I could use it for the cover of this book.

Out and about

I distinguish stones, glass and crystals from less desirable elements by:

- Assessing the object's weight in the palm of my hand; glass, crystal and stone are heavy compared to plastics.
- Putting it to my cheek or upper lip to determine if it's cool; plastics tend to be room temperature.
- Tapping the item against my teeth; glass, crystal and stones click while plastics *thud*.

To determine if pearls are real, I rub them lightly against my front teeth; genuine pearls feel gritty.

These methods aren't elegant (or hygienic), but they're effective.

Garage sales

They can be outstanding. In Michigan I paid $10 for a big wood drawer filled with 1940s medical and sewing supplies.

I sold most of the items from my shop, but the most unusual piece was an antique tape measure in the shape of a turtle; the reptile's tail was the end of the tape and you pulled to measure. *It was adorable.*

Research showed it was very old and very rare, worth about $800. I rarely aimed for book value then (and wouldn't dream of it now). I listed for less – which was still *extreme* profit – and it easily sold online.

Resale Shops

Most of the resale and "charity" shops are on to us; they've hired people who are fairly knowledgeable. Some price their goods as high as antique shops.

In Oakland County (Michigan) I went to my favorite Salvation Army on Mondays because Sunday's donations were just hitting the shelves. They also had "sale color for the week" posted on the board.

Methods vary, so – if you're serious about buying right – know how they operate and make it part of your routine.

Jewelry-related finds

Most of the time I look for vintage jewelry, especially pendants and chains. Ignore them as a set because the chain might be perfect for a pendant you already have; or the pendant might be better suited to a different chain.

Look for staging elements that may help you take better photos, including:

- Earring holders and jewelry boxes
- Luxurious satin, velvet and lace fabrics; they can be cut from vintage skirts, dresses and lingerie

Make sure the prop's design doesn't distract or detract from your merchandise.

Don't leave home without your loupe

I saw a Russian-looking religious print in an 80s frame; upon closer inspection I found the print was more than 100 years old. I put it in an age and style appropriate frame and sold it for many times the purchase price.

Look low, look high

I spotted a hint of color among old frying pans on a bottom shelf. When I knelt for a closer look, I found a stack of stunning antique plates had been stashed out of view.

The price was low and that day they were *half off!* I sold them out of my shop. But now my sales are online, so I usually pass on dishes. They're fragile, heavy and expensive to ship. I don't bother unless they're exceptional.

I do occasionally find nice porcelain. A few years ago I discovered an old vase on a top shelf at Goodwill; *think pale pink and yellow hand-painted roses, baby blue trim with gold edges and handles.* It was only $3.

I collected hand-painted porcelain for many years. I knew what it was before I turned it over – "Hand Painted Nippon." (Produced from 1891 to 1921)

What is Nippon?

According to the International Nippon Collectors Club (www.nipponcollectorsclub.com):

"'Nippon' literally translates to 'Japan'. This porcelain was made specifically to be exported to the west with designs and patterns that suited American's tastes."

I used to have a nice collection, but I sold it; so this vase was a gift from the universe. Unfortunately, someone wrote the price on the fine white bottom in *black magic marker.*

I googled and found toothpaste will (usually) remove marker from porcelain, dolls, plates, etc. Apply a small amount, wait a few minutes and wipe gently with a damp cloth. If it's not completely gone, repeat.

Goo Gone will remove residue from self-adhesive tags.

FLEA MARKETS

Flea markets are thriving little communities where you can *never* make assumptions of social status based on clothes or vehicle. The grizzly guy in the dirty jeans and rusted pickup might own the best antique shop in town.

When you go to the same market several times, you *will* be noticed and you *will* establish a reputation among the dealers. If you're accepted, you can expect great deals, knowledgeable assistance and valuable information about other prime hunting grounds.

When to go

My parents have been antique dealers for many years. My mother believes in getting there before the crowds; she has been known to shop at 5 a.m. by flashlight.

My stepdad likes to go late and negotiate with sellers who hate the thought of packing it all back up.

What to bring

Take pen and paper so you can make a quick map of what's where.

Also take:

- Twice as much cash as you think you'll need
- Your debit card in case you didn't bring enough cash
- Lightweight bags and/or a foldable cart with wheels
- Field/price guides; or do quick searches on your smartphone
- Business cards for establishing contacts

If the flea market is small, cruise through quickly to see what's there; you can always go back.

Negotiating

Bargaining is expected, but you never want to make an insulting offer.

In my experience, 20% is a reasonable target. Sometimes prices lower further as you turn to walk away. Watch the more respectful buyers on Market Warriors to see how it's done.

One dealer told me about a woman who made a lowball offer on antique porcelain.

She said "I'll give you twenty dollars for that."

He said "It's a steal at $50."

They went back and forth and she insisted "I WILL GIVE YOU TWENTY!" He held the piece straight out in the palm of his hand, flipped it and said "No you won't!"

His dramatic message – "I would rather destroy it than sell it to you."

CHAPTER 16: MARKETING YOUR ONLINE BUSINESS

When we're proud of what we're doing, it's only natural that we would want to tell the world.

I exist in multiple forms on Facebook - a personal page, a marketing writer page, a page for this book and others. On my book page I share favorite finds with friends and poke fun at the awful ones. I recently added a link to a heart-shaped *dog tag* (with current address and phone number) that had been listed as a *love token*!

FACEBOOK

A Facebook presence will help you establish yourself as a serious dealer. You might use a name similar to (or the same as) your eBay User ID; simply follow the directions.

Your main photo should be an outstanding representation of your merchandise and the background photo should complement, not compete.

When you post a link or eBay listing to Facebook, a photo from the page (usually) appears.

In this case I was nervous/excited about sending jewelry to Russia.

BLOGGING

Consider sharing your activities on a blog as well. Setup is easy and it's free; I like wordpress.com.

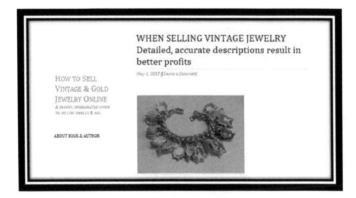

Use your eBay seller name or think up a new one that encompasses the whole of what you sell. Boil it down to two or three words like "Fabulous Fobs" or "Celtic Coins" ... you'll see why shortly.

Buy a domain name

Those words I asked you to play with? Go to Godaddy.com to see if they're available as a domain name. *Examples:* fabulousfobs.com or celticcoins.com

Always go for the most respected extensions – .com, .net or .org. If they're not available, consider tweaking the name.

Domains only cost $10 to $12 per year, but you must be ready to buy the first time around; if you don't, GoDaddy will raise the price.

Within a few minutes you can "manage" your newly purchased domain. Simply "forward" it to your blog's URL and you'll be able to refer friends and customers to *yoursite.com*.

Choose a template

WordPress has a nice variety of template designs; you can change them any time without losing your work.

Generate content

Write about what you're learning, buying and selling. You can also create a quick blog about a great book or article and link to it. Take time to add categories, search terms and tags; that's how your blog will be found.

Promote your efforts

Every time you post a new blog, announce it with a link on Facebook; and add your new web address to your email signature line and business cards. (I like vistaprint.com)

CHAPTER 17: SELLING BIG STUFF

If you've inherited a house full of goods, it might be best to hire a professional to conduct an estate sale. Check credentials and get the specifics in writing.

If you choose to do everything yourself – *and I don't blame you one bit* – you need to know what your merchandise is worth.

PRICING

Start online. A Google search may yield pricing information from recent auction sales.

eBay: Search under "Antiques" – "Furniture." Get acquainted with the values and note the shipping methods sellers use.

To see what's happening locally, choose "More refinements" and "Item Location;" here you have an ability to choose within so many miles of your zip code.

Craigslist: It's a freak show, but it doesn't hurt to check it for prices, pictures and descriptions. The nice thing about Craigslist is you can compare values in other cities/communities.

Antique shops and shows: Prices are high at both. Shop owners have to pay mortgage or rent, displays, utilities, employees, taxes and more. Dealers at shows are paying rent and the cost of displays.

Consider their prices your best case scenario and know that they will usually discount 10 to 20%; especially if the buyer flaunts cash.

Reference books: I no longer depend on collector & reference books for prices; they're good for identification and details, but that's about it.

Things fall in and out of favor and some preferences are local.

TAKING PHOTOS

There's no need to stage large items, just remove distractions (garbage cans, kitty litter trays, etc.) and make sure everything a prospective buyer sees is clean and inviting.

Take photos every which way – front, back, sides, insides and top.

(This antique wicker chair looks better from behind.)

Drawers, nails and construction methods speak volumes about the age of a piece. In some cases, look underneath.

You're hoping to find old labels, stamps and marks; you may not know what you have, but collectors will.

Take photos of damage and remember that most people don't expect old furnishings to be perfect.

(This wicker chair is a bit gimpy, front right.)

Pictures and prints

Glare is an issue. You may be able to remove the glass without damaging the print; in most cases I leave them as is and shoot outside in indirect light.

SELLING LOCALLY

In southwest Florida I don't see much antique furniture going through eBay.

The best options seem to be posting to Craigslist, putting an ad in the newspaper or having a garage sale. In all three cases, you're allowing strangers onto your property, so be careful.

Craigslist

Craig started his list in San Francisco in 1995. It's free, it's local and it's often the best way to sell your larger possessions.

Buyers like it because they don't have to pay shipping fees. Sellers like it because it reaches a large audience and you can maintain anonymity until you have a serious buyer on the hook.

In the past few years I sold a sideboard, a huge piece of stained glass, chairs, several antique beds and assorted bulky items. In most cases I didn't get as much as I wanted, but I don't think I could have made more any other way.

I recommend proceeding like this:

- Search for similar items before you place the ad; learn from their headlines, details and photos.
- Include your location in the headline.
- Insist on cash.
- Protect your privacy.

Don't post your address or phone number – make them respond through the automated and anonymous email function. It's a great screening device.

If the potential buyer can't manage an email, you don't want them in your house.

I ask a friend to help me move the object to my front door so buyers have no reason to come in. (Most buyers have been women.)

(I love my 80s headboard, but the footboard was a waste of space; so I sold it.)

Newspaper ads

Choose a popular local paper and watch your word count. You don't need a lot of words to write an informative ad. Include essentials like:

- Age or period
- Weight; in some cases – as in antique wicker – this can be an indication of age
- Color or type of wood
- Size or dimensions
- Condition
- Price
- Contact information – phone and/or email

Example: "Heavy Victorian metal bed frame, twin, some rust, $200 OBO; 888-888-8888."

154

I prefer email to phone, so my ad would read: "Heavy Victorian metal bed frame, twin, some rust, $200 OBO; myname@yahoo.com"

I usually place ads on Fridays, expecting most people have free time on weekends.

If the first person to come out gives you a lowball offer, don't fall for it. That is SO predatory. Take their number and say you'll call if you change your mind.

Garage sales

Check to see if you need a permit; then gather (or make a list of) everything you want to sell.

If you don't have enough, contact friends, family and neighbors and see if they have anything they'd like to add to your mix. (Maybe you can convince one or two to help out.)

Advertise your garage sale on Craigslist (garage sales are under *for sale*) and/or in the paper.

Craigslist is great because you can add photos. Include day, time, location and type of merchandise in the heading.

Example: Sunday 9:30-3:30 Victorian furniture, primitives and glass (Fort Myers)

Label your merchandise.

If several people are selling their wares, make sure labels are initialed.

You may want to write prices on press-on labels and add a layer of clear tape to thwart tag switchers and label peelers.

Have cash on hand for change.

About $95.00 should do it.

- 2 – 20s
- 2 – 10s
- 4 – 5s
- 10 – 1s
- $5 in quarters, times, nickels and pennies.

Consider buying a receipt book so you can provide dealers with a record of the transaction.

Put sturdy signs out at major crossroads

Include:

- ANTIQUES in huge letters
- Street and address in big letters
- Directional arrow
- Hours ("Sat 10-5")

You may want to designate parking areas to keep strangers off the neighbor's tulips.

Handling the leftovers

Some people make the last day "Clearance Day" and discount *everything.* Others donate the debris to charities and take receipts for their contributions.

CHAPTER 18: SETTING UP SHOP

If you want to generate income with little effort, you could consider hooking up with a good consignment shop. If you're willing to work, you could rent space at a flea market, do antique shows or rent space in an antique mall.

Flea markets

I've been tempted to try this. I imagine mobile credit card readers make things a lot easier than they used to be.

Antique shows

I haven't had the stamina to do shows, but I've heard great things. A Michigan dealer told me antique shows are days of wheeling and dealing followed by nights of libations, campfires and camaraderie. It's a simple matter of finding out where they are and requesting specifics.

Antique malls

Renting space in a mall is a great way to ease into the business. All you have to do is find a shop you like and ask:

- How much is the rent?
- Do you have to work the shop a few days ever week? Some places give you a choice; rent is usually higher if you don't work.
- Can customers pay by credit card? (Sales are better in shops that do.)
- Which area would be yours?
- Is it well lit, conveniently located and attractive?
- How often will you be paid?
- What types of sales reports are provided?
- Do they have carts and easy access to loading areas?
- Would you have access when it's closed?

Some shops are so trusting they'll give you your own key.

True Story: **My First Mall**

In the nineties I worked with a bright, bossy graphic designer who knew I loved antiques. We were driving through Royal Oak, Michigan, when Jennifer started pointing out shops.

She said "I know one that has space to rent. You should start selling your stuff!"

It was a tall brick Victorian building. The front window was artfully arranged with oriental rugs, primitives and pottery. We walked through and the variety was outstanding.

I called the number on the window and the rest was easy. I worked one day every other week and it was all cash and checks, no credit cards. Money and receipts went into a box.

Every two weeks the owner divided earnings into white envelopes and left them for us to pick up at our convenience. She took a modest percentage of sales.

It was fun. I made a little bit of money, learned restoration tricks from more experienced dealers and antiques started to seem like a hobby with financial potential.

It occurred to me that the real way to make money was to open a mall and rent to dealers. As the years passed, I rented space in various places, opened my own shop, rented to dealers and ultimately went solo.

And then I got sick.

Like John Lennon said, "Life is what happens to you while you're busy making other plans."

In Conclusion

Selling online is a satisfying creative enterprise that can offer fun, adventure and extra income.

I love that we *never* stop learning.

Do you have questions? Did I leave something out?

Please join me on Facebook at "How to Sell Vintage & Gold Jewelry Online."

(Princess on the lanai; protecting us from squirrels)

~ Namaste ~

Made in the USA
Middletown, DE
15 August 2018